CRYSTAL ENLIGHTENMENT

The Transforming Properties
of
Crystals and Healing Stones

Volume 1

First published in 1985 by:
Aurora Press
205 Third Avenue, Suite 2A
New York, N.Y. 10003

ISBN: 0-943358-27-2
Library of Congress Catalogue No: 85-071008

© Cover Photograph—Crystal Vision Inc.,
Royal, Arkansas
Art Director—"Crystal Bill" Kaunitz
Photographer—Bill Disney
Courtesy of Richard Berger,
Crystal Resources, N.Y., N.Y.

CRYSTAL ENLIGHTENMENT

The Transforming Properties
of
Crystals and Healing Stones

Volume 1

KATRINA RAPHAELL

AURORA PRESS

205 Third Avenue   2A   New York, N.Y. 10003

TABLE OF CONTENTS

PREFACE

The crystal story has many versions and numerous authors. Legends and folklore date back to the beginning of the human race, when it was believed that crystal forces set the electromagnetic field of the earth so that human souls could incarnate. Legends of the ancient continent of Atlantis tell us that crystals generated power for entire cities, and it was the abuse of these energies that resulted in the eventual destruction of that civilization. Some Egyptologists speculate that the magnificent Egyptian pyramids were capped with crystals to channel cosmic forces into these geometrically perfected structures. Many civilizations, cultures and peoples have used crystals and stones for a myriad of purposes—from healing and protection to the most powerful initiations.

The purpose of this book is to share a small portion of that sacred knowledge so that the beauty and light inherent within the crystal kingdom may continue to be shared and utilized by those who are instinctively drawn to it.

The information in this book was received through personal attunement and meditation with the stones over several years' time. I worked very closely with my dear and wonderful friend, JaneAnn Dow. For over a year we would meet once a week in her home and meditate in her office which housed hundreds of beautiful crystals and healing stones. We chose the stones we wanted to learn from, closed our eyes and tuned into the energies and information that was available to us. Our sessions were recorded and later transcribed by JaneAnn. We would then find ourselves in the kitchen eating ice cream or taking delight in other such decadence—then off I would go. It was not until later when I was reviewing our transcripts to prepare for a crystal healing class I was going to teach, that I became fully aware of the valuable information that had been shared from the crystals. It became evident that anyone who wished should have access and be able to use the information we had been blessed to receive. Thus it was agreed to write a book, to completely cover the bulk of the material. I am very grateful to JaneAnn for her continued support, love, friendship and collaboration which helped create and complete this book.

Undertaking such a project was overwhelming and I had doubts whether my time and energy could accommodate such a massive commitment. Surrendering to the divine will, I boldly stated to the Universe, "If this book is meant to be, give me a sign and let me know that the world wants and needs this information." It was less than a week later when Barbara Somerfield of Aurora Press came to my home to buy a crystal and ended up saying she would finance and publish *Crystal Enlightenment*. It was the sign I had been waiting for, and I began writing immediately. Translating the material from the original transcripts into a language that could be easily read and interpreted was a long (six rough drafts) but worthwhile task; one that assisted my own growth immensely. A year and many changes later, it is my privilege to present this knowledge to you. May it serve you well.

This book in no way claims to be the only way or the final word about crystals. It remains forever open to the revision of higher truth. This book is for those who are drawn to it, in whose hearts it tests true on the inner touchstone. It is my prayer that the knowledge in this book be used for personal and planetary betterment—and that the light within the crystals and stones serves to draw each one closer to his/her own inner source of light.

Crystal Enlightenment is designed for the lay person, as well as the professional, to give the basic understanding necessary to use the healing properties inherent within the mineral kingdom. There will always be more to learn and experience once you open up to this incredible world of light. Enjoy the reading, and receive some of the secrets we have obtained from the stones. Open your mind; accept and integrate into your being that which rings true. That which does not, release without being judgmental. Remember that if you ever want to be shown the truth, or gain clearer perspective, you can place a crystal to your brow; close your eyes; will it; and know.

CHAPTER I

INTRODUCTION TO THE MINERAL-CRYSTAL KINGDOM

Minerals and crystals are different things to different people. They can be a source of income, a gift for a loved one, a decoration, an appreciation of nature, a tool in healing, a symbol of perfection, or a teacher in consciousness. The mineral kingdom will serve each individual need in the way that can best be accepted by that individual. To some, crystals and stones are inanimate objects, the lowest form of life on the planet. To others, they are great sources of light and energy. In whatever way they serve, these beautiful gifts from the earth bring pleasure to the eye of the beholder as they display exquisite colors, perfected geometric forms and radiance into the lives of millions. Before you decide what crystals are for you, let's take a closer look and discover more about them. (When referring to crystals, we are not speaking of the man-made lead crystals that usually hang

1

in windows and create rainbows of color on the walls. Instead, we are referring to the natural crystalline forms that are grown within the Mother Earth).

WHAT ARE CRYSTALS, PSYCHICALLY AND ESOTERICALLY?

Like all matter, crystals are composed of minute particles called atoms. These building blocks of the physical plane are made up of even smaller particles called protons, neutrons, and electrons. When examined very closely, these basic units of energy are not really matter at all, but subtle vibrations, each being attuned to the cosmic force. The entire physical world is created from different variations and combinations of these atoms. The way in which the individual atoms join together with other atoms determines what molecules will form and what materials will manifest. In the formation of crystalline structures, such as clear quartz, the atoms join together in perfect unity and harmony, as if they were holding hands or mutually coming together as in a jigsaw puzzle. This primal integrity also manifests on a molecular level as all of the pulsating molecules vibrate at the same frequency. This micro-structure (or lattice) determines the physical properties of the crystal: its outer shape, hardness, cleavage, type of fracture, specific gravity and optical properties.

In the crystal kingdom there are seven families. Each family has its own geometric structure and molecular similarity, and each has its own lineage of crystals that form from the common geometrical lattice. Individ-

2

ual crystals will externally manifest to the naked eye the inner molecular makeup and cosmic geometric design. Each crystal system has its own imaginary axis of rotation and different angles at which the axes intersect. The lengths of the axes and the angles between them define the crystal's shape. The seven tribes of the crystal kingdom are: The Isometric System (cubic, such as fluorite), Tetragonal (four-sided, such as wulfenite), Hexagonal (six-sided, such as emerald), Trigonal (three-sided, such as quartz), Orthorhombic (lozenge-shaped, such as topaz), Monoclinic (singly inclined, such as azurite) and Trilinic (thrice inclined, such as turquoise). These seven primal crystalline categories are natural universal designs that manifest on the earth plane through the crystal kingdom.

The orderly way in which the atoms arrange themselves in any crystalline structure is what makes these material forms whole and complete unto themselves. Each individual unit of energy aligns itself with the cosmic force and then harmoniously joins with its fellow atoms to create a very purified form of matter. This physical manifestation of unity vibrates with the cosmic harmony that created it. In so doing, perfected forms, brilliant colors, and radiant light can be witnessed and experienced. The terminated peak of the crystal connects and aligns each molecule, atom, proton, neutron and electron that comprises the crystal to the universal source of infinite energy. Crystals are capable of receiving, containing, projecting, emanating, refracting and reflecting light, which is the highest form of energy known in the physical universe.

When crystals, or anything in the material world is explored in its atomic make-up, it becomes obvious that

3

the entire physical manifestation is but a vibrational variation of one primal essence. When the scope of conscious vision expands to see reality in this way, the limitations of the mind are transcended and the doors to the higher dimensions and inner planes swing wide open. Crystals can assist in the active awakening process by showing and teaching us how to align ourselves with that essence which creates and comprises the entire universe.

HOW ARE CRYSTALS FORMED?

Nearly all crystals are created by the repetitive addition of new matter to a growing crystalline mass. Some crystals have their origin in the magma or fiery gases of the earth's interior or in the volcanic lava streams which reach the earth's surace. These minerals, which include quartz, are called magmatic or igneous. They form by the solidification of this molten material as it cools and hardens. As the molten rock mass cools, the atoms group together to form the essential regularity which determines the shape and composition of the crystal.

Some crystals grow from vapors in vents in volcanic regions. This type of crystal includes sulfur and is condensed from hot mineralized gases into a solid state as the vapors are escaping from the inner earth.

Some crystals form from water solutions or grow with the help of organisms on or near the earth's surface. These crystals are known as sedimentary minerals and are formed through the process of mechanical or chemical weathering. Air, water, wind and ice are the main erosion factors involved in dissolving the earth's materials that will eventually be cemented together and occasionally crystallize. Such is the case with calcite.

Lastly, new minerals are formed by the recrystallization of existing minerals under great pressure and high temperatures in the lower regions of the earth's crust. These metamorphic minerals undergo structural and chemical changes after the original formation. These changes will reorganize the atoms, creating different textures, compositions and crystals. An example of a metamorphic mineral is garnet.

No one really knows how long it takes for most crystals to form. Some speculate that it takes thousands of years, others say that when the elements are right, crystals could form in an instant. Whatever is Mother Nature's secret, she conceives, incubates and gives birth to a wide variety of exquisitely beautiful crystalline forms.

HOW ARE CRYSTALS MINED?

There are two main types of mineral deposits in which crystals are found and mined. The first is from rich veins in the earth, which are channels or spaces in other rocks through which mineral-laden solutions are deposited and crystallized. Crystals which grow in veins can be mined by amateurs with the simple tools of a hammer and chisel or in large scale operations with expensive explosives and equipment. Large quantities of crystals are usually found in hollow spaces within the earth which provide the freedom and room for growth. It is sometimes necessary to follow a vein deep into the ground by drilling and blasting in order to mine hundreds of pounds of crystals. Quartz crystals are mined in this way.

The second method of mining is performed to retrieve crystals which have been concentrated in deposits in beach or stream beds. These placer deposits are composed of fragments of decomposed veins which may contain such crystalline delights as topaz or diamonds. The most common method of mining placer deposits is to shake sieves of crystal bearing gravel under water to separate the heavier gravel from the crystals. Once separated, the crystals can then be easily seen and picked out. This type of mining is usually done on a small scale but the process can be duplicated to accommodate large scale mining operations as well.

In order to bring out their innate beauty after being mined, crystals often need to be cleaned with strong chemicals. Once prepared, the crystals will then find themselves in the proper mineral shops or gem shows and be attracted to exactly the right person.

THE ART OF FASHIONING CRYSTALS AND STONES

Some crystalline forms are further cut, shaped and polished by lapidary artists who specialize in bringing the highest quality, luster, and color to the crystal or stone. Most transparent gem stones, such as rubies, emeralds, or diamonds, are faceted by cutting the stone at different angles to improve and enhance the physical and optical properties. Each facet enables the stone to capture more light which will be internally reflected, displaying the stone's innate depth and color. This process involves time, training and machinery and will increase the beauty and value of the gem.

Some stones are cut into simple flat-based domed shapes called cabachons. This process allows many semi-precious or flawed precious stones (such as garnet) to be lightened in color and increased in value for use as jewelry or as healing stones.

Smaller rough stones can be tumbled until the stones are smooth and free from surface imperfections. A tumbler is a simple machine which is rotated by motor at about forty revolutions per minute with finer and finer grades of grit. The total tumbling process takes anywhere from five to eight weeks, depending on the hardness of the materials being polished. Tumbling increases the beauty and radiance of stones that might otherwise go unnoticed or unappreciated. Tumbled stones, such as rose quartz, are small enough to carry, beautiful enough to give or to wear, powerful enough to use in crystal healings and inexpensive enough to afford.

When stones are treated in any of these man-made ways they usually end up reflecting greater light and color. In this way, we as humans, assist in the evolutionary process of the mineral kingdom. A lapidary artist that is attuned to the stones that he works with can create entities that will inherit a healing essence and beauty that honors both the artist and the stone. A skilled artist can take a rough unappealing stone and transform it into a precious jewel that can reflect high amounts of light and healing energy, contributing to the growth process of both the stone and the persons using it.

CRYSTAL HISTORY: PAST, PRESENT AND FUTURE USES OF CRYSTALS AND HEALING STONES

Down through the ages, civilizations have used the power of crystals and stones for many purposes. The oldest legends and lore of crystal magic lead us back to the ancient continent of Atlantis. It is supposed that the evolved inhabitants of this advanced race used crystals to channel and harness the cosmic force. This legendary civilization of advanced sciences would use crystals as beacons of light that would serve as a telepathic communicator to their universal forefathers. They also used crystal power for many physical and practical purposes. It is believed that one of the reasons this great continent was destroyed was because this sacred knowledge was abused and the awesome power misused for egocentric purposes. It is rumored that before Atlantis was destroyed, the uncorrupted wise ones wished to preserve the knowledge the race had inherited. They dared not transcribe it into books for fear that throughout the earth's cataclysmic changes the records would be destroyed. In their wisdom, they programmed certain crystals with the information and rematerialized them into the earth. They trusted that when the time was right these crystals would surface on the planet and be attracted to the people who could attune their minds to receive the wisdom stored within (see Record Keeper).

The survivors of Atlantis began anew and continued to perpetuate the knowledge of crystals in Egypt, South America and Tibet. They built pyramids using crystalline theories and patterning them after the great temples in Atlantis. The pyramids' perfect geometric form duplicates the laws of crystal physics and channels high frequency universal energy onto the planet. It is believed that the Great Pyramid in Egypt was originally capped with a giant crystal to assist in the grounding and utilization of this cosmic force.

As the root civilizations rose and fell, the latent knowledge of the power and potential of crystal energy was hidden from those who were corrupt in their motives. Much of the wisdom has been lost but some of the information has survived and sprouted in different cultures and civilizations throughout history.

It is recorded in Exodus in the Bible that a breast plate made of twelve precious jewels, combined specifically together in four rows, and worn over the heart would endow Aaron with the power of God. Although it is not known what specific stones were used in the construction of the breast plate, it is recorded as being divinely inspired and having incredible spiritual powers.

Kings in ancient India were advised to collect the very best gems to protect themselves from harm. Early works on astrology, written in Sanskrit and dating back as early as 400 B.C., make elaborate observations on the origin and power of stones. In those days astrologers advised people struck with misfortune to wear different kinds of stones to counteract the negative effect of the planets. (This philosophy is the foundational belief upon which the Astrological Trinities Chart was created; see page 156.)

Medical practices of many ancient cultures included wearing talismans and amulets around the neck. Depending upon the ailment, specific stones were worn to bring about the desired effect. Old Rome believed that external objects, such as stones, had a direct and positive influence on the body. Early references in Greek and Roman writings indicate that stones were worn as talismans for health, protection and to attract virtues.

Throughout history gems and stones have been associated with royal blood and were elegantly worn in crowns and jewelry, embedded in thrones, laid in swords and used as decorations in other treasures. Many deceased royalty were laid to rest with elaborate collections of gems and stones. When the tomb of King Tut of Egypt was found, the array of riches astonished the world!

Mayan and American Indians have used crystals for diagnosis as well as for the treatment of disease. Large clear quartz crystals were used in special ceremonies by the elders of the American Indian villages as "seeing crystals" in which images of the future or distant events could be seen. Certain tribes of Mexican Indians believed that if you lived a good life, your soul went into a crystal when you died. If someone was fortunate enough to find that crystal, it would speak directly to their heart, heal, guide and make their dreams come true.

Different cultures and peoples have utilized the power within crystals and stones for as long as humans have inhabited the earth. They have been used in a myriad of ways and purposes. Today, with the rapid advancement of technology, crystals are being used to transmit and magnify energies in many different ways. Ruby crystals, both naturally formed and man-made, are being used in lasers for microscopic surgery. Each year thousands of pounds of quartz crystals are being mined and crushed to be used for technological purposes. Quartz crystals are used in ultrasound devices, in watches, and as memory chips in computers. Quartz is used as oscillators for controlling radio frequencies in electronic equipment; as capacitors to modify energy capacity in circuits; as transducers to transmit energy from one system to another and as condensers that will store energy.

On a more esoteric level, stones and crystals can be used in meditation to develop the intuition and learn from the higher senses. Crystals or stones can be placed under the pillow during sleep to inspire lofty and prophetic dreams. They can be used in healing practices to stabilize erratic emotions, soothe troubled minds and help heal body imbalances. They can be held during the labor and birth process for added strength, used in ceremonial rituals, or placed around plants, animals or children who are in need of balancing or healing.

The power and potential of crystals cannot be overstated. It is one of the main contributors to the New Age and can and will be used in many forms for many purposes. The material contained in this book is part of a sacred knowledge on how to use crystals and stones for healing and advancement of consciousness. These teachings are for everyone and can be applied by anyone who is intuitively drawn or attracted to such information. Caution must be taken when using the power of crystals and stones in this way. This knowledge is only now, after thousands of years, again being made available to humankind. Intentions must be humanitarianly pure or the powers could be severely turned against the abuser. The information contained in this book (or any other book on crystal power) is to be used only in accordance with divine law and as a means to transform the human predicament and usher in the Golden Age of Aquarius.

The time is now when once again the healers and lightworkers will step forth and use the crystals and stones as tools in bringing onto the earth a new ray, a new way and a new race. Crystals and stones are very much a part of the planetary transformation of which we are *all* a part. In whatever way you choose to use them, use them ethically and consciously.

CHAPTER II
WORKING WITH CRYSTALS

TUNING IN

The art of attunement to a crystal, to oneself, to another person, or to any aspect of life, is one of the most valuable tools that can be learned. Tuning in is the ability to neutralize the mind and become so still that the inner self can perceive the truth. By learning the art of attunement, we not only develop the sensitivity necessary to attain valuable inner information, but we also train the mind to communicate on much more subtle levels with different life forms. When one tunes into a crystal, the crystal becomes a mirror that will reflect the light within back into the consciousness. Meditation, visualization, physical exercise, yoga, prayer, or personal techniques can be used to calm the mind to achieve clearer perception. Whatever the approach, the results speak for themselves: greater self-control, more inner peace, personal connection to the source of truth, and the ability to have access to information that otherwise might be unavailable. Crystals can be powerful tools and teachers in the attunement process. They speak their own special language that can be interpreted if the listener possesses a clear mind and an open heart. The evolutionary process of crystals has been much different than human evolvement, and they can share the secrets of their creation and reality.

Crystals are there for anyone and everyone who chooses to work with them. They easily become teachers and friends as they share their knowledge and secrets and lend their light and radiance for our healing. All it takes is an openness and willingness to listen to their silent voice as it speaks directly to your inner knowing. Crystals are representatives of the light and if attuned to correctly can teach us how to gain access to and use more of our own light.

Have you ever listened carefully to hear a special secret from a very important friend? That is how you open your mind and heart to communicate with crystals and healing stones. Drop any preconceived notions, expectations, or fears that it cannot be done, and allow the inner mind to receive the subtle impressions that the crystal will emanate. Open yourself to the possibility that these crystalline life forms want to share their secrets and wisdom with you. Accept without doubt the spontaneous images that come into consciousness. As the mind is trained to listen and communicate in silence, responses will come quickly and clearly as the light and energy of the stones you are working with reflect your own wisdom back to you.

A method that has always worked for me is to practice yoga and meditation for at least an hour. Then I lie face up and place a crystal at my third eye point. As relaxation occurs and the mind becomes receptive, the subtle vibrations of the crystal can be felt. At this time you may want to ask the crystal if there is anything that could be shown to you to assist in your understanding, or you may want to ask a personal question concerning some aspect of your life. Ask the crystal to reflect the answers from the truth within you into your conscious awareness. Then open your mind and receive the answer. It may come in symbols, images, visions, or direct knowing. However it comes, know it is a message from yourself to yourself amplified and relayed through the crystal with love. It is possible through this procedure to realize many things that you have not understood, come to know yourself on much deeper levels, and to have access to greater sources of inner power and strength.

Get to know each one of your crystals and healing stones and learn what their unique secrets are. They may be different for you than for anyone else, as the stones will attune themselves to serve and respond to whoever is using them. By assisting your stones to serve their purposes, you are also helping them to evolve and fulfill their higher destiny. It is not until humans mine crystals and stones from within the earth that they are exposed to the sun's light, thereby allowing their beauty and color to be revealed. In return, the stones become tools for our healing. By working consciously with the mineral kingdom, you learn how to better express your own inner light while helping the crystals to express theirs. We are on this earth together to serve each other, that each may grow, and in doing so, work in greater harmony to create a better world.

HOW TO USE CRYSTALS AND HEALING STONES

There are many ways that crystals and stones can be used for healing and consciousness raising. They will work whether or not you think or believe that they work. Just having them in your presence brings more beauty and light into your environment. If crystals are sitting on a dresser, coffee table, or nightstand they will automatically charge the area with energy, much like a negative ionizer. If an argument has taken place in a room, a crystal can be placed in the area to purify the vibrations and restore peace. All the crystal needs to do is be present to bring more light and healing energy to an environment. As light is reflected through and off of the crystals, energy is created that serves to neutralize any negative vibrations and raise the overall frequency to one of greater harmony.

If someone has not yet reached the stage where he has developed the sensitivity necessary to feel the healing energies of crystals, the effect of the crystal's energies will still be accomplished and the subconscious mind will respond. The mere presence of crystals in an environment suggests subliminally to the subconscious mind that perfection is possible. The crystals prove to the physical senses that it is a reality to be clear, beautiful, focused and radiant with light. If nurtured, these seeds planted within the subconscious will eventually sprout and blossom. Therefore, it can be beneficial to give crystals and stones even to those who are not aware or do not care about their healing properties.

Jewelry

Crystals and stones can be carried or worn as jewelry to help you maintain mental clarity, emotional stability and physical balance. Carrying stones as amulets, or wearing them as jewelry, is one of the most simple and effective ways of utilizing their healing force. Gems have been worn for thousands of years on the fingers, around the wrist and neck, in the navel and on the third eye, in the hair, on the toes and through the nose. Beautiful stones and crystals have been used as jewelry for as long as people have adorned themselves. Lapis, carnelian and malachite were used by the ancient Egyptians, emerald by the Incas, jade by the Chinese, and turquoise by the American Indians. Many of these great cultures were aware of the healing power in the stones; they would use them consciously for specific healing purposes. Crowns of sacred gemstones were worn by the rulers of great empires to assist them in governing the people wisely. Stones were worn on specific fingers to channel certain energies and influences into their lives. Rubies and deep red stones were worn in the navel of belly dancers to activate sexual interest in their viewers. Stones were worn on the third eye center to assist the ascetic's consciousness to stay attuned to God. Necklaces hanging in the vicinity of the chest were worn to stimulate heart chakra points in order to activate greater love and compassion; and stones worn on earlobes were used to stimulate reflex points that affect other parts of the body.

Much of the knowledge of the real purpose for the creation of jewelry has been lost. Originally stones that were believed to possess certain energies were carried and kept close to the person wishing to acquire its specific influence. Eventually stones were secured with twine or string and hung around the neck, wrists, head or ankles and worn against the body in order to receive full-time effects. Once again, in recent times, many minds are becoming aware of the specific energies inherent within the nature of stones that, when combined in certain patterns and so worn, will create healing and rejuvenating effects.

When jewelry is designed and worn consciously for healing purposes, the creations become works of art that empower the wearer. As crystals and stones are worn, their energies intermingle with the human electromagnetic field or aura. As light responds to the stones and the color vibrations are reflected back into the aura, the increased color frequencies serve to dissipate and neutralize psychic and emotional stress. By increasing the subtle healing energies and light force around the body, greater personal power and balance is achieved.

In addition to cosmetic beauty, it is also possible to create jewelry that consciously utilizes the healing properties and the special gifts stones have to offer. These creations, uniquely designed, then become personal power pieces that will assist the wearer to attain certain states of awareness or achieve specific goals.

Remedies

Crystal remedies are easily made and can be taken when it is not possible to carry or wear the stones that are needed for specific results. They can also be taken to increase the effects of the stones that are being worn or worked with. Place cleansed stones or crystals in a pure lead crystal glass, half-filled with distilled water, and place it in the morning sun for three hours preferably from 8–11 A.M. when the day is fresh and new. As the sun reflects through the liquid and into the stones, the water becomes charged with the vibrational force and color frequency of the stones. This potent elixir can then be put into sterilized eyedropper bottles and labeled to be used when needed. For best results, take five drops in a glass of water or directly under the tongue several times a day, as you visualize the stones and affirm their healing qualities. To make a permanent stock and preserve the remedies indefinitely, it is recommended that the eyedropper bottles be filled half way with alcohol. (High quality brandy is preferable.) The best stones to use in remedies are the multi-colored quartz family: clear, amethyst, rose, citrine and smoky. Quartz responds favorably to the light and water remedy method, as well as offers a complete color spectrum of effects. Caution should be taken when choosing stones and crystals for remedies for internal use. Some stones, such as realgar for example, contain a high content of arsenic.

Crystals or healing stones can be placed in massage oils or topical ointments. A close friend, who has practiced massage therapy for several years, has always kept a beautiful green tourmaline wand in his massage oil for an added healing effect in his treatments.

Love Gifts

Crystals and stones make one of the most special gifts that can be given. When given in love they become forever "love-crystals" and symbols of that special caring. They can still be used as healing crystals—indeed they have been charged with the very force of healing. Before they are given, hold the crystal to your heart. Do a meditation, and visualize the person you are giving it to as being well, balanced, whole and happy. This impression will be programmed into the stone, which will emanate that energy for as long as it is with the receiver.

Personal Use Stones

As your friendship and love for the crystals grow, you may find yourself in special places where they are sold. Keep an eye out for one that sends you a special beam, one that psychically tells you that it is to be used especially by you for personal purposes. This stone may become a constant travel companion or can be worn or carried with you: it can even become an assistant in healing practices or as a meditation partner. Only a very special and unique crystal can be used in this way and would best be kept as a private stone, possibly untouched by others. This type of personalized crystal usually comes to you in such a manner that you know, without a doubt, that it is a powerful personal tool. You will know when your talisman crystal comes. But even then lay no claim. On occasion, after such crystals have served your purpose, it is time for them to travel on—on to other places and other people in order to share their light and healing energy. It then beomes necessary to let go and learn to work with the crystals telepathically. I would like to share an experience that taught me this very important lesson.

I walked into my home to find that it had been broken into and ransacked. Among the things that were stolen were some of my finest healing stones. I had used those stones every day in crystal healings and could not understand why they had been taken from me when they were truly loved and used in service. In anger that my precious tools had been taken, I was tempted to immediately telepathically program the stones to wreak havoc in the life of whoever had stolen them. But I knew the karmic repercussions of doing such a thing was not in harmony with the healing vibrations of the stones. In a meditation I sat with a large selenite crystal and a black obsidian ball and asked to be shown why this event had taken place and what my personal lessons were in experiencing this loss. The answer came quickly and was very clear; the stones had been charged with healing energy from the work that had been done with them, and they were ready to go out into the world to be with people who really needed their light. I was then shown that the stones would find themselves into the lives of people who would recognize their power and healing force—probably children. Whoever came in contact with the stones would in some subtle way be affected and healed. My opportunity was to continue to work with the stones by mentally connecting myself to their energy and sending thoughts of peace and prayers of love, for whoever they were with. In this way a bridging of light could occur, and the stones would serve as interconnecting points. The stones would be further charged by my conscious attunement. The stones had their higher purpose and were fulfilling it. I would fulfill mine by beaming positive thoughts of peace into the stones. When the meditation was over, I very respectfully thanked the selenite and obsidian ball. Thus, I realized that our reality is created by how we interpret the events in our lives. Even a potentially very negative occurrence could be altered to serve the light. Now in my meditations and prayers I tune into those stones that I love and know so well and I feel confident that my projections are being received and put to good use.

Crystal Meditations

Any healing stone or crystal can be used as a meditation partner. It may be held or worn during meditation in order for you to absorb its specific properties. Crystals or stones also may be placed within visual range to be used for mental focusing. Thus, they serve as symbolic concentration objects. They may be placed upon the heart chakra for emotional balance, or to the brow for mental clarity. You may find a crystal that specifically communicates that its purpose is to deepen and strengthen your meditations. Or, you may want to experiment with the various ways different stones affect your meditations.

Clear quartz is one of the crystals that is used to stimulate the crown chakra (the highest energy in the body, located at the top of the head). By lying face-up and placing the terminated point of a clear quartz crystal (the apex where the facets have naturally grown together to form a peak) at the top of the head, the higher consciousness centers are vibrated and a state of greater awareness is achieved. During this meditation there would be an added result if an amethyst crystal were placed at the brow to still the mind, and citrine at the navel to ground the experience into physical reality.

Programming

For any meditative result a clear quartz can be programmed by projecting a thought into it and holding it during meditation. For example, if you are experiencing anxiety about an interview or an examination, hold the terminated point of a clear quartz up to the third eye center and visualize yourself as being calm, secure, confident, and spontaneously flowing with the situation. Project this thought form into the crystal and then sit quietly, holding the crystal, as you mentally reaffirm to yourself the positive reality you have created. This crystal can then be carried with you, to be held, looked at, or thought of during the event for which you have prepared. The crystal retains the programmed thought form and will emanate that vision back to you, acting as an assistant and friend.

If you have reason to ask for an answer to a specific question, ask and then place a clear, single, double-terminated, (both ends naturally coming to a point) quartz crystal to the third eye center and see the solution in your mind's eye. If you have need to send loving thoughts or prayers to another person, place the crystal pointing out from the heart chakra, visualize the desired result and project the image through the crystal to be received by the person for whom you pray. If this person is very sensitive, he/she will feel the vibrations you are sending. In this way you can establish a conscious telepathic link. If the person is not aware of the healing vibrations you are sending, the effects will still be received and utilized by the subconscious mind. If ever you want to use the same crystal to program different thoughts, it is best to cleanse it after each projection (see care and cleansing of stones, page 26).

Crystal Enlightenment

There is an advanced meditation that can be done with clear quartz that requires mental stillness and concentrated focus to experience the full results. In this meditation, you experience what it is like to be a crystal. Start by sitting, with the spine straight, holding one of your favorite meditation crystals in the left hand for several minutes. Close your eyes and become totally receptive to the impulses sent by the crystal. Put it next to your navel, heart and brow to feel its vibrations; then place it within close visual range. Stare into it for several minutes: close your eyes and take the image of the crystal into your mind. As your consciousness moves into the crystal, observe its molecular structure. The crystal is a purified form of matter. Notice that all of the molecules are combined in absolutely geometric constructs (i.e., no random ordering). All of the molecules are vibrating at the same frequency. With advanced meditative practice, it is possible to expand your awareness to encompass each molecule, each atom within the molecule, and each electron within the atom. Witness that each material component is vibrating in unison with all of the rest and expressing a harmony beyond its own individual volition. Allow yourself to surrender and experience within your own being the cosmic frequency and attunement in which the crystal exists. As you merge into this bliss, you may experience a harmony and peace with yourself and all of creation. It will be as if time and space have been suspended. You are simply blending into a cosmic resonancy and continuing to pulsate in a state of being at one with the universe. Within this nucleus of yourself, truth resounds. The truth of any and all matters can be made known by learning how to settle your consciousness into your own nuclei, your center, the silence. Once this reality has been established, it then becomes your touchstone and sacred sanctuary—accessible to you at any time. At this stage of the meditation it is important to breathe deeply in order to maintain conscious connection with the physical body and to channel your state of peace and attunement into the material reality. To complete the meditation, envision the crystal with golden rays of sunlight passing through it and radiating from it. Now see yourself as the crystal, being synchronized with the cosmic harmony. Thus you, too, can become an instrument of the light of the universe. Feel yourself being totally clear and luminescent, empowered by your own personal source of light. When practicing this meditation, it is beneficial to have a smokey quartz or a piece of black tourmaline available to hold when you open your eyes. These stones will ground the experience of expanded consciousness into the body. It may also be good to carry those dark stones with you for several hours after this meditation to ensure proper integration of energies.

Group Healing Meditations

Group healing meditations can be done with a large single quartz generator crystal (six to 40 inches). These clear large generator crystals are rare and usually very expensive. They are often located in environments where they can be used by conscious people in healing circles. It is best to have at least three people to do this type of meditation. Place the crystal in an upright position in the center of the circle with each member of the circle pointing a smaller quartz crystal at the large generator. At this time, either mentally project or verbally state positive affirmations for personal, interpersonal, or planetary healing. These projections are intensified by the crystal being held and directed towards the large generator crystal which beams the conscious projections into the ethers to affect the causal plane (refer to glossary). After the prayers and projections are sent, turn the termination of the crystal you are holding towards the heart center to receive personal information or healing energy. End this meditation by sharing among the group personal responses and sensations experienced by working with such a powerful energy generator.

CARE AND CLEANSING OF STONES AND CRYSTALS

Like anything else, crystals and stones like to be treated in a manner that is respectful and loving. They enjoy being in plain sight where they can reflect their light and radiate their beauty. There was a time that I stored crystals that I was selling underneath a covered table in my home. When I would pull the tray of crystals out from underneath the table I would get the sense that they were not happy being kept in a darkened area on the floor. One time when I pulled them out I got the direct message that they wanted to be placed in the light where they could be seen, appreciated, and able to do their work. I responded and placed them in every nook and cranny that I could find. Doing this filled my environment with more light and the crystals sold much faster because their vibrant energy was obvious to everyone that entered my home. Since that time, I would never consider keeping crystals or healing stones in a space that was not worthy of their presence. They love to be in window sills, on top of shelves, on bedstands, counters, desks, meditation altars, tables, fireplaces, in plants or anywhere that they can serve their purpose.

When transporting stones or travelling with them it is best to have them individually wrapped so they don't become damaged or chipped (unless they are small tumbled stones). Small satin, silk, leather, velvet or cotton pouches are excellent carrying cases for stones.

Unless crystals and stones are being used directly in healing practices they will usually not need to be cleansed. It is suggested, however, that when crystals are first purchased or received, they be cleansed to clear any vibrations they may have accumulated in their travels. Cleansing also resets their vibration to be receptive to the new home and owner. It is best to cleanse new stones by submerging them in sea salt for at least three hours before using them for healing or personal purposes.

RECHARGING

When crystals and stones are used for healing purposes, they become very receptive to the vibrations of the individuals that they are working with. They can pick up and retain their energies and therefore should be cleansed after each treatment. Often times, however, if the individual receiving the crystal healing is consciously participating in their healing process, the stones actually can become energized and will not need special cleansing. In these cases the stones can be kept in a well lighted room (preferably sunlight) or on a large quartz cluster to receive ample cleansing and recharging. If, however, an individual is in need of deep healing or is unwilling or unable to actively take part in his/her own healing process, it is likely that the stones will give much of their own light and energy to aid in the healing. In contributing so much they can become drained of their own vital forces and, in these cases, should be cleansed and re-energized before being used again. When crystals or stones are in need of purifying they often lose their radiance and become dull and clouded. As you work with crystal healing and get to know the unique energy of each of your healing stones, you will be able to easily tell which stones need more intense cleansing.

There are several ways to effectively cleanse and recharge crystals and healing stones. One of the most simple ways is to use the healing forces of nature by utilizing the rejuvenating properties of the sun and water. In this method the stones or crystals are held in the hand as cool water is poured over them (it is also possible to hold them under a running tap or faucet). Then place them in the sun (preferably outside) and allow the sun's rays to shine through them for at least thirty minutes. Afterwards gently polish the stones with a clean white cotton cloth. If you are fortunate enough to live by the ocean, a lake, or a fresh water stream, this method can be used as the active motion of natural waters runs over them, purifying and recharging. Then continue with a sunlight bath and polishing. Crystals and stones love to be in natural environments and waters. It is therefore advised to hold on tightly while cleansing them in rapidly moving water, for it is not unlikely that they would prefer to stay there and jump out of your hands, never to be seen again!

Working With Crystals

For general cleansing and recharging one can use a clear quartz cluster and four single terminated quartz crystals. Stones in need of cleansing are placed upon the cluster with the four single quartz placed with the terminated end pointing towards the cluster. Create a cross formation around the cluster by placing the single crystals in north, south, east and west directions. In this way the single points charge the cluster which in turn recharges the stones. Stones can be left on the cluster for an indefinite amount of time, possibly even becoming the home for the stones in between crystal healings. Quartz clusters themselves rarely need cleansing due to the intense light reflection off of the multi-terminated points which creates a force field that is self-energizing. If, however, you sense that the cluster does require cleansing, the water-sun method is best to use.

If you choose to personally recharge your special stones or ones that need quality attention, hold them in your right hand, close your eyes, and send your own healing energy into them. Envision a beam of brilliant white light entering through the top of your head, connecting with the love at your heart chakra and then extending down your arm into your hand into the stone. If you choose, you can visualize a thermometer-type scale with numbers on it from one to ten. As you concentrate on channeling healing light into the stone see the light rise up the scale until it reaches ten, then maintain it there for at least three minutes. In this way you can recharge stones that you frequently work with with your own healing energy. Energizing stones in this fashion programs them not only with your own personal essence but also with the power of universal white light. Stones that are worked with often in this way can increase their healing power up to ten times, becoming more beautiful and radiant than they were originally.

Stones or crystals that have become exceptionally drained or have been misused can be cleansed by submerging them in salt (preferably sea salt). Fill a clear glass or crystal bowl with salt, completely bury the stone in the salt and leave it for three days. The salt will neutralize the negative charge and draw out the impurities, restoring harmony and balance to the stone. Upon removing the stone from the salt, rinse it in cool water and let it dry in the sun. The salt should be disposed of and not reused. At times it may be necessary to cleanse stones in several different ways if they are very polluted or depleted. For example, a friend had sprained her ankle and we placed a small malachite stone under the ace bandage to draw out the pain. After about twelve hours her ankle was almost healed but the malachite stone was practically dead from absorbing so much trauma. It had become dull and lifeless and had lost all of its ability to reflect light. The small malachite stone went immediately into intensive care and it was several months before it recovered. First it was submerged in salt for three days, then cleansed with the water-sun method, then personally charged, and finally took up residence on a beautiful clear quartz cluster. The stone is still not as vibrant as it was, and probably never will be, but it served to teach me the lesson that it is not possible for a small little malachite stone to take on such a big healing and survive the challenge.

CHAPTER III

THE ANCIENT ART OF LAYING ON STONES

When the physical body shows signs of dis-ease the true reasons for it are often hidden. Suppressed or unresolved mental and emotional conflicts can surface and manifest in the physical body. These seeds of emotional upset and mental stress are often sown long before the body displays symptoms of imbalance.

As children grow up there are many experiences that can cause confusion and hurt feelings. Unable to process or understand the reasons for life events, a child will often suppress and store away these unpleasant feelings somewhere inside himself. Sooner or later these unresolved conflicts will show up in attitudes, belief systems, destructive habits and physical imbalances. The body becomes a storehouse of outdated, misunderstood and unresolved events. Different parts of the body tend to retain specific types of emotions: the heart and lungs register sorrow and grief; the liver stores anger; the stomach anxiety and fear. These impressions are also recorded in the auric energy field surrounding the body. When old thoughtforms or past emotional conflicts cloud the aura, it becomes difficult for the inner light to radiate and be expressed. This can make a person even more vulnerable to negative internal or environmental influences.

In the process of healing dis-ease it is important not to look only at the physical symptoms but also the underlying mental and emotional causes. Until now there have only been a few methods that could effectively treat the more subtle mind/heart blockages. Now with the knowledge of the healing power of stones, the physical, psychic and emotional bodies can be healed and aligned with the source of life energy-spirit.

Crystal healing, through the art of laying on stones, is one of the most advanced and effective methods of cleansing the aura, releasing suppressed traumas, and connecting a person with his/her own source of truth and power. The power to change and heal, to learn the lessons inherent in life events; the power to forgive and let go, and to make conscious decisions; the power to exercise compassion and patience; and most of all, the power to love one's self: all these can be claimed and owned once the old patterns are released. Crystals and stones assist in this self-empowering process by increasing the amount of light present in the aura which stimulates and activates the more powerful subtle realms of being.

In the practice of crystal healing, the stones become crystalized light forms that are placed onto vital nerve centers, chakra areas and plexus points on the body. The stones act as a catalyst to perpetuate and integrate more color and light into the subtle energies of the human aura. This increased energy frequency serves to dissolve and dissipate the dark shadows of suppressed or unreleased pain that cloud the aura, confuse the mind and dis-ease the body. The crystals can neutralize this negative charge and energy is released from the mental-physical blockages. The transforming power of the stones recirculates that energy to its source, to be used for conscious purpose. It is then the responsibility of the individual receiving the healing to let go of the old and receive the new energy, using it to recreate a positive identity based in self-love and inner truth. This then becomes the foundation upon which dreams are built and visions lived.

Once the stones are laid upon the body it is possible for old memories and feelings to surface and be expressed. In treating the real cause of dis-ease, it is likely that trauma dating back to childhood, birth, pre-birth, or past lives will be remembered as these experiences resurface to be learned from and neutralized. As feelings are traced back to their source, it is important to assist your partner to breathe deeply as you guide him/her to visualize the image of light and healing energy entering on the inhale and the stress and pain being released on the exhale. As the light is consciously focused upon, it becomes possible for the soul's intuition to communicate to the mind why those experiences were necessary and chosen and what lessons are involved. With a greater perspective and understanding it is then possible to let go of old patterns and replace them with positive affirmations and visualizations that, in turn, will create a new physical reality. This conscious reprogramming process is one of the most powerful tools towards self-change and personal empowerment.

All crystal healings are not cleansing in nature. As the aura is infused with light and color from the stones, it is possible for open, sensitive people to experience altered states of awareness. Visions, colors, past life recall, or future occurrences can be witnessed as the crystals and the human energies blend and the consciousness expands. For people who are not emotionally congested, crystal healings become an opportunity to utilize the stones' energy for conscious creative purpose.

The purpose and intention of practicing crystal healing is to assist those whom you work with to neutralize, balance and align the physical, mental and emotional bodies so that they can tap into their own inner resource of power and truth. True healing occurs when one accepts full responsibility for him/herself and in so doing, claims the power to heal. The crystal healer and the stones are light-workers assisting in the process by sharing their attunement, love and healing energy. The role of the crystal healer is to assist others in clearing and opening their channels to consciously experience their higher selves.

PREPARATION

It is suggested that before performing crystal healings and laying on of stones, the practitioner prepare beforehand by attuning with the stones and crystals in meditation. Align yourself with the healing energies of the stones, and become receptive to their frequencies. Crystals and stones should always be used with respect and acknowledgment of their forces. Tremendous power can be generated when the stones and crystals blend with the human aura and an energy exchange takes place. (The first time I did a crystal healing with someone I was unprepared for the influx of increased energy frequency and almost lost consciousness. I had to leave my client alone for several minutes in order to regain my composure.) It is important to visually surround yourself with light and mentally affirm that you are working in, tune with the energies of the stones to harmonize, balance and heal.

Crystal healing requires constant conscious focus. Many subtle changes take place in the auric field as the stones clear blockages and dissolve emotional debris. It is important to remain sensitive to, and aware of, the responses that the receiver may display. Observe the heart rate by watching the throat pulse. It may increase in speed as the body's metabolism adjusts to the added auric energy. If the breathing becomes shallow, direct your client to breathe deeply and completely in order to integrate the increased energy into the physical system. Develop your third-eye sight so that you can perceive the aura, the chakra system and the higher subtle energy frequencies.

At times it may be necessary to remove certain stones if your clients are unable to integrate the higher frequency energies into their auras. Therefore, it is important to also stay in-tune with the stones. If you are not attuned to remove them, do not be surprised if the stones bounce off by themselves. Be aware of how much your stones can give without being depleted, and be prepared to remove them if they begin to be drained. Be able to spontaneously respond to the messages your stones will relay to you. If the person you are working with is actively participating in the healing process, the stones usually get charged in the process. But if the person you are working with will not accept responsibility for his/her own healing process, the stones can be drained of their vital forces, becoming dull and clouded. Stones such as malachite, which absorbs negative energies, may need to be purified after each use. Your personal attunement to the person with whom you are working and to your healing stones will insure a successful treatment and positive results.

CRYSTAL HEALING LAYOUTS

My co-workers and I have used the following layouts with great success in crystal healing sessions. These layouts are fairly new and revolutionary in our present time, but they are ancient in evolutionary practices. Following each crystal healing it is suggested a mirror be available so that the recipient can see the layout and visually affirm the beautiful energies of the stones.

General Layout

This type of layout can incorporate the use of any number and kind of crystals or healing stones. The stones can be placed upon the chakra centers or on top of any area that may be congested or imbalanced. This treatment is approached spontaneously to meet specific needs of the client. There were times that I would have certain preconceived images about the layout of stones for a particular person before a session. But once I actually became tuned-in to the person and the stones, what I had formerly envisioned was often incorrect. It then became necessary to let go of my expectations and become open and intuitive to the moment in order to fully meet the needs of my client.

Up to a hundred different stones can be used in one crystal healing if the stones are placed properly and in a manner that will balance and align the subtle and physical energies. Beautiful patterns and designs can be created to direct the flow of energies.

Generally speaking, at least one corresponding stone would be placed upon the chakra points with other stones surrounding it to create the desired effects and energy flow. However, there may be an occasion to work with only one area or chakra center. Be creative in fulfilling the need at hand.

The type of result you are trying to achieve will determine the stones that should be used over specific areas. For example, if a client is very meditative but not very grounded or able to function well on the physical plane, stones in the red-orange spectrum can be placed upon the navel area with dark or black stones patterning down to the pubic area and legs. With a proper balance of blue-purple stones on the forehead, a flow of energy is created that assists in integrating the peaceful meditative state into physical manifestation. It is also beneficial to work above the body with a small (two to six inches) generator quartz crystal to direct energy downward from the crown to the groin. On the other hand, if someone is self-centered and earthbound, a large variety of clear, gold, blue, purple, and pink stones can be placed upon the chest and upper forehead to stimulate the higher consciousness centers. Ground these effects on the physical plane by placing at least one gold-orange stone at the navel and a dark stone at the pubic bone. Again, direct the flow of energy through the aura with a single terminated quartz crystal.

This type of treatment allows for complete creativity and spontaneous intuitive action. Have all of your healing stones and crystals present, and be aware of the stones that vibrate or radiate to let you know when they are to be used. Keep attuned to your clients and guide them to direct their own breath and healing energy into the areas that require balancing. Have active communication and encourage verbal expression and sharing.

The manner in which the stones are removed is usually not in the same order as they were laid on. Again, work in accordance with the stones and remove them as you are intuitively guided. Wipe each stone with a damp cotton cloth as you take it off and set aside the ones that may need cleansing.

Basic Energy Charge

This is one of the most simple layouts. It is done with three small clear quartz clusters and two small single terminated quartz generator crystals. With the receiver lying face up, a small cluster is placed upon the center of the brow, one on the center of the chest and one at the navel. This will energize the consciousness, activate the heart chakra and stimulate the physical systems. Hold one of the single generator crystals at the top of the head while you slowly move the other crystal in a straight line from the pubic bone to eventually meet with the one held at the crown. As the moving crystal is passed through the aura (two to six inches above the body) be sensitive to feel any congestion or energy blockage. Consciously direct white light energy from the crown generator to meet with the moving crystal; keep it charged with enough light force to dissolve any auric debris. Then visualize a flow of energy moving from the crystal at the crown to all other parts of the physical and auric bodies. As the moving crystal passes over the clusters on the navel, heart and brow, direct a beam of healing energy through the generator to further charge these centers. When the moving crystal can pass through the aura without sensing any blockage or energy congestion, the crystal healing has served its purpose. Crystals may be removed in the order in which they were placed.

Chakra Balance Layout

This layout can be done with any group of seven stones that correspond to the color frequencies of the seven chakras (see stones/color/chakra chart, page 162). Crystals in the quartz family are very effective in this layout for they manifest the colors of several of the chakras. A sample layout would be as follows. Point a single quartz crystal at the top of the head; place an amethyst on the third eye, aquamarine at the throat, rose quartz at the heart, malachite on the solar plexus, citrine quartz on the navel and smoky quartz on the pubic bone. Stones should be placed in a direct line and a single generator quartz passed two to six inches above the stones to balance and align the chakras. Be open and sensitive to feel where energy is imbalanced, creating excess energy in one chakra and depletion in another. Project your healing force through the generator crystal to direct the excess energy to feed the depletion. Other stones can be placed around the main chakra stones to accentuate the healing force. For example, if the heart chakra was blocked because of emotional trauma, green aventurine stones could be placed above and below the rose quartz with pink/green tourmaline pieces to be sides. If the purpose of the healing is to direct suppressed emotion into verbal expression in order to be released, single terminated clear quartz crystals can be placed upon the sternum pointing towards the throat, directing the energy from the heart to the throat to be expressed. Any number of stones can be used in the chakra balance layout. Study the effects of each of the stones and select the ones that will produce the results required in each individual case.

Chakra Charge Layout

This layout is specifically designed to energize a particular chakra. Nine single clear quartz crystals are used. To begin, place a clear quartz in each hand of the receiver (termination directed towards the shoulders). Place one pointing at the instep of each foot and one pointing at the top of the head. These five crystals form a star shape around the body that will create a protective force field and allow the increased energy to be recirculated into the person's auric field. The other four (preferably smaller) quartz crystals are placed on the body with the terminations directed inwards towards the chakra that needs charging. One can be placed in a north position, one in the south, one in the east and west, creating a cross configuration. An advanced method of this layout would incorporate a stone that corresponds to the chakra. The chakra stone should be placed in the center of the cross. For example, if you charge the heart chakra, a rose quartz or pink tourmaline piece is placed in the center of the chest, with the quartz crystals pointing towards it. Further energizing occurs if a generator crystal is held over the center stone with healing energy being projected and directed through it. If the center stones used are amethyst (for the third eye), citrine (for the navel), or smoky quartz (for the first chakra), a single crystal of the same kind could be worked with in the aura above the chakra stone. Several chakras can be energized in one session by simply changing the center stones and replacing the four single quartz to surround it. This is a powerful layout and should be practiced only if an individual is in need of charging his/her energy centers.

Pink Tourmaline Spiral

This layout is specifically for those who wish to release deep emotional pains. It is especially beneficial to use when the physical body has already manifested that pain in the form of dis-eases such as cancer, asthma, bronchitis, or other such illnesses. At least six pieces of pink/green tourmaline are placed in a spiral rotation clockwise around the heart chakra. If tourmaline wands are used, the terminations are placed outwards, towards the arms. At least one tourmaline wand is needed to hold and move in a spiral motion above the placed stones. As the wand moves in a clockwise direction spiralling up through the aura around the heart chakra, suppressed emotional energies are released. This layout can also create emotional releases (crying, anger, etc.), and the practitioner should be prepared to counsel or care for the person receiving the healing. To balance this state, place black tourmaline pieces on the lower chakras or groin area. Most physical dis-ease has its roots in deep emotional hurt. The electrical healing properties of pink/green tourmaline vibrate these pains at a frequency that will release them. The green initiates the healing while the pink ushers in love to replace the old hurt.

Fluorite Octahedron Layout

This layout is done with seven Fluorite Octahedrons, three larger and the other four smaller, preferably of equal size. Place one of the larger ones in the center of the forehead with the point of the triangle touching the hairline and the base towards the eyebrows. Place two of the smaller octahedrons above the center of each eyebrow, triangles pointing towards the larger octahedron in the center of the forehead. Place another large one at the throat, triangle directed towards the hcad, and a large one on the navel, triangle pointing towards the feet. Place the remaining smaller octahedrons in the center of each groin (where the legs meet the lower abdomen) with the triangles towards the feet. Allow the stones to remain in these positions for at least 11 minutes while the receiver breathes deeply and tries to calm the mind by releasing each thought as it enters the consciousness, ushering the mind into a state of neutrality and peace.

This layout is designed to channel and ground cosmic energy into the creative centers of the human body The large octahedron at the hairline directs higher frequencies of energy into the consciousness centers of the brain while the smaller octahedrons at the eyebrows balance the hemispheres of the brain, allowing this to occur. The large octahedron at the throat activates this verbal creative center, allowing higher consciousness to be expressed through the spoken word. The large one at the navel directs those higher forces into the physical body to be integrated into the actions of day to day life. The small fluorite octahedrons on the groin further ground and stabilize these forces into the physical body.

This layout, if practiced with regularity, will neutralize the thought processes, enabling the mind to consciously touch the source of all knowledge, which is spirit. When the mind surrenders and lets go, it can then merge into a higher form and become the pure creative force which is the essence of all thought. Upon tapping into this infinite reservoir of creative energy, it is then possible to consciously create the thoughts that will produce the desired results in one's life. This can only occur when the mind surrenders and truly humbles itself to cross over the threshold into the unknown, the inconceivable. Upon doing so, the resources for conscious creative thought are abundant. The Fluorite Octahedron Layout, if practiced once or twice a week for six consecutive weeks, will initiate and continue to develop these advanced mental faculties.

CHAPTER IV

THE NEW AGE STONES

We are on the threshold of a new age, the Aquarian Age. The decisions that we make today will determine the heritage of our children's tomorrow. By the year 2000 the future history of the earth will be etherically written. It is the responsibility of each individual inhabiting the earth at this time to make a decision—probably the most important choice in life. The question presented before each one of us is, "Are you willing to let go of past outdated belief systems, programming, concepts and ideologies that no longer serve the force of life and growth in order to embrace, incorporate and integrate the laws of love into the very fiber of your being? Are you willing to live those laws courageously in every aspect of your life?" If enough people have the integrity of character to totally commit and devote themselves to living and sharing more love, then our earth can reverse the destructive probability that awaits the human race if this choice is not made.

Crystal Enlightenment

As an aide to the potentially turbulent and determining years ahead, the New Age Stones, along with the knowledge of how to use their forces successfully, have emerged to help reverse the course of human self-destruction and ensure planetary peace. The New Age Stones are willing to contribute their light force and reflect their beauty in assisting us to take the most important step in the course of human history, and safely cross the threshold into the Aquarian Age.

As we learn to attune ourselves to the subtle and powerful effects that light and color have on the human psyche and on the energy systems of the body, we will move into a new and more advanced system of health care. This New Age healing approach will include the mental, emotional, spiritual and past life influences of an individual's dis-ease and successfully treat the sources of human illness. This approach will result in the complete balance and wellness to the whole person. As we progress into the New Age, crystals and healing stones will be used more frequently and with increasing success to remedy the causes of all types of illness.

These specialty New Age Stones are specifically for this day and age and for the people who suffer with the myriad mental, emotional and physical problems inherited from the influences and energies typical to our times. The New Age Stones have come to reflect possibilities in consciousness and lifestyle, to give us an alternative by providing us with the color, light and beauty that the soul intuitively responds to. As the soul force is nurtured and developed, we will become immune to the many negative influences that intrude upon our minds and bodies and be able to focus all of our attention upon peace, love, growth, prosperity and happiness for all.

Many of the New Age Stones reflect colors that our minds are only now ready and capable of perceiving. Some of these stones have only recently been discovered and some are only now, after thousands of years, willing to disclose their secrets and offer their healing energies to the world. It is a special and blessed time to be alive and to have the opportunity to join forces with these stones to create a world that will inhabit conscious, loving, whole, exuberant beings.

The following chapter is devoted to sharing the stories that I have personally witnessed and experienced while working with the twelve New Age Stones. As you work with and harness the forces of these very special stones you, too, will notice their healing and transformative influence in your life, as well as in the lives of those who share in their healing vibrations.

THE QUARTZ FAMILY

Quartz is one of the most common minerals on the earth and has the largest variety of specimens which display an entire panoramic spectrum of color. Not all of these diverse forms of quartz will be explored in this book, but I would like to mention and appreciate their presence as valuable members of the quartz family and as perhaps an invitation for your further study.

Agate	various colors, can be banded or layered
Amethyst	violet, pale red-violet
Aventurine	green, gold-brown, iridescent

Basanite	velvet black
Blue Quartz	dull blue
Carnelian	flesh-red to red-brown
Carnelian—Onyx	red base with a white upper layer
Chalcedony	bluish, white, gray
Citrine	light yellow to gold-brown
Crysoprase	green, apple green
Dendritic Agate	white-gray and translucent with fern like images
Flint	opaque and dull colors
Fossilized Wood	gray, brown or red
Hawk's Eye	blue-gray to blue-green
Heliotrope, Bloodstone	dark green with red spots
Jasper	all colors, mostly striped or spotted
Moss Agate	colorless with green inclusions
Onyx	black base with a white upper layer
Opal	opalescent precious opals, yellow red fire opals and common opal
Prase	leek-green
Prasiolite	leek-green
Quartz Cat's Eye	white, gray, green, yellow, brown
Rock Crystal	white to colorless

Rose Quartz	strong pink to pale pink
Sard	red-brown
Sard-Onyx	brown base with a white upper layer
Smoky Quartz	brown to black, smoky gray
Star Quartz	rock crystal showing a star when polished
Tigers Eye	gold-yellow to gold-brown

Clear Quartz Crystals

When most people talk about crystals, they are usually referring to clear quartz. This type of crystal is the most common and well known and could be related to as "the grandfather" of the mineral kingdom. Generally speaking, clear quartz can be used for all purposes as it vibrates the clear white light which contains all other colors.

Quartz is the salt of the earth and is indigenous to this planet. It is comprised of silicon dioxide which is one of the earth's most common mineral compounds. It is interesting to note that human beings are also largely comprised of silicon dioxide. Would this make us cousins of different kingdoms in the family of earth?

Quartz crystals represent the sum total of material plane evolution. The six sides of the quartz crystal symbolize the six chakras with the termination being the crown; that which connects one with the infinite. Most quartz crystals have a flat base which was their roots to the earth. Oftentimes quartz are cloudy or milky at the bottom and gain more clarity as they reach the terminated peak. This also symbolizes a similar growth pattern in which the cloudiness and dullness of consciousness is cleared as we grow closer to the point of union with our infinite self. Clear Quartz Crystals prove that the material plane can and does reach a state of physical perfection capable of containing and reflecting pure white light. Clear Quartz Crystals are a symbol of coming into alignment with cosmic harmony. They demonstrate that purity and unity in every molecule and atom of their being. Clear quartz radiates with divine white light and by seeing, touching, wearing, using or meditating with these crystals one can actually work with that light in a physical form.

The Clear Quartz Crystals that one attracts into one's life are stones that in some way will facilitate that particular person's growth of awareness. To unawakened minds, they will work subliminally through the subconscious. For the aware souls who are walking upon this planet, crystals will be like beacons that will add more light and positive energy to be used in their lives and integrated onto the earth. Quartz crystals represent perfected material form, aligned and harmonized with the cosmic force. They are much like the pyramids in that they channel high frequency energy onto the physical earth plane. Clear Quartz Crystals reflect pure white light that can be channeled into daily thoughts, feelings, words, and actions. They stimulate the finer, more subtle realms of our being which can then be integrated and manifested into our lives.

The evolution of the quartz crystal is much different than ours in many ways, and very similar in others.

The New Age Stones

Quartz crystals are conceived within the womb of the earth and matured there until they are born onto the surface of the planet, much in the same way that humans incubate within the warmth of the maternal womb while grounding their spirit into a physical body before entering the material world. Each crystal is unique and unlike any others, each with its own personality, lessons and experiences, (as with humans). The purpose and destiny of both is to unite with cosmic consciousness and manifest that on the material plane. Crystals and humans can become working partners in that process and serve each other's evolution. When the mineral kingdom and the human kingdom link their forces together, new worlds of consciousness unfold. As the healing essence of quartz crystals vibrate the soul of humanity, vast hoizons of hope and joy appear.

Quartz has the remarkable ability to vibrate its energy at all of the color frequencies, from black to yellow, green to pink, and on into the blue and purple spectrum. In this way, quartz demonstrates how to manifest the clarity and purity of white light into denser and lower frequencies. This ability to be multi-colorful can teach us how to vibrate all of our seven chakra centers simultaneously while maintaining perfect alignment with the light. This is the ultimate challenge of being in a physical form; to fully utilize all creative centers while consciously expressing the multi-faceted use of light.

All things are light and varying degrees of light manifesting in color. In quartz crystals the light force merges with the physical plane elements, blending different tones and vibrations together, creating beautiful colors. This light and color is what allows the healing process to occur. Quartz crystals vibrate the aura at such a high rate that the darker tones of karmic seeds can be dissolved and released. Quartz crystals then return that energy to its source to create higher vibrations and brighter colors to be recirculated into the aura. This type of deep soul healing can strengthen the inner depths of one's being and build a strong foundation on which to stand and live.

Within Clear Quartz Crystals are usually found clouded areas or inclusions. Sometimes they resemble galaxies, which indeed they are. These crystals show us that worlds exist within worlds and that the creation is limitless and unfathomable. This realization immediately inspires an awe and respect for the infinite creative force which all forms of life humble themselves before.

Many quartz crystals have reached a completion of evolution and will not change much once they have been midwifed onto the surface of the planet. These crystals carry within them their own unique markings which relate their identity, stories, records and information. However, some quartz crystals carry clouds within them that can be cleared as the crystal evolves and grows beyond its limitations. These crystals, after being used in crystal healings, meditations or continuously worn, can become perfectly clear and sometimes change beyond recognition. They will change as the person who is working with them clears their cloudiness of consciousness and transforms it into clarity. These crystals have parallel lessons and will reflect the changes as they occur within the crystal and the individual working with it. As crystals are worked with and attuned to, it will be possible to know what the inner markings of each crystal contains and what each individual crystal's potential and possibilities are.

There are many different ways that Clear Quartz manifests and can be worked with. This holds true for the entire quartz family. The following quartz summaries describe some of the unique and fascinating forms in which you may find quartz crystals revealing their nature.

Generator Crystals

Generator crystals are clear single quartz crystals that can be used to channel and ground pure healing energy. Six natural facets join sharply together to form the terminated apex. The crystal is supported by six sides and grounds the light force at the base. These crystals may be cloudy at the bottom and clear at the top, reflecting rainbows, displaying phantoms, with intricate inclusions, or completely clear. Each Single Generator Crystal is its own entity, each carrying its own story and its own experiences and lessons. Generator Crystals have great individual personalities and easily become good friends and associates in healing. Single Generator Crystals can teach us how to concentrate, focus, and magnify our own healing energy. These crystals demonstrate with their example how to channel the radiant light force into our beings and onto our world.

Generator Crystals are an example of a physical structure that is pure enough to beam white light onto the physical plane. Generator Crystals are just that—generators of cosmic force. Their perfected geometric form allows for the focus and proper distribution of this energy into the lives of the people working with them and receiving their healing energy. Generators also intensify and direct the healer's energy as it is channeled through the crystals. Generator Crystals are ideal to use in meditation or crystal healings. They can be used in layouts to direct the flow of energy from one chakra to the next. Simply direct the termination of the crystal in the direction in which you want the energy to flow. Generator Crystals can also be held directly above the chakra points to purify and recharge the energy centers (also see Crystal Healing Layouts, Chapter 3).

Generator Crystals can be as small as ¼ inch or as large as three feet. They can be carried with you or placed in the most obvious or sacred of places. They are power pieces and should always be used with respect and knowledge.

Clear Quartz Single Generator Crystals are the most common and clearly state with their presence the ability we all have to be clear, focused and directed in the expression of light. Single terminated Amethyst, Citrine or Smoky Quartz are also Generator Crystals, each channeling its own particular essence. For example, Amethyst would channel the purple ray of devotion and be ideal to use over the third eye center.

Generator Crystals are also in the process of evolution. As they are tuned into and worked with, it is very possible that they will become clearer, brighter and capable of carrying more light.

Crystal Clusters

Clusters are formations of single terminated crystals that share a common base. Clusters are many individual crystals who all live together in harmony and peace. They represent the evolved community, each member being individually perfect and unique yet sharing a common ground, a common truth, with all the others. In clusters, all units join together to reap the benefits of living, learning and sharing in an advanced society. The individual crystals reflect light back and forth to one another and all bathe in the combined radiance of the whole. The auric light that surrounds the quartz cluster is very bright and strong.

These crystals can be placed in areas in which you want to create a stronger healing vibration or in places where you want to cleanse the atmosphere. For example, if an argument has taken place in a certain room, quartz clusters could be placed in that area to purify the environment of negative energies and feelings. Clusters can also be placed in between two people, in meditation, to gain greater harmony with one another.

To purify and recharge healing stones, crystals, or jewelry, place them upon large clusters for at least three hours. Pictures of friends or family can be placed upon, or next to, quartz clusters to direct a ray of positive energy towards loved ones throughout the day and night. Clusters can also be used directly over the chakra centers to dissolve any negative or unwanted influences. This enables one to connect with their own source of light and balance themself.

There may be hundreds of single terminated points in a quartz cluster, or there may only be two. Small clusters are ideal to use in crystal healing layouts (see Basic Energy Charge, page 38), while larger ones usually find homes on altars, desks, counter tops, window sills, bedstands, or any place where they can reflect their radiance. Clusters are wonderful gifts to homes where the occupants need to harmonize and cooperate.

Most popular and accessible are Clear Quartz clusters, but equally as beautiful are clusters of other members of the quartz family. Other minerals such as Fluorite or Wulfinite also form exquisite cluster formations. If nothing else, clusters are an incredible work of beauty in nature and extremely pleasurable for the senses, as well as the soul, to behold.

Double Terminated Crystals

When the six faces of quartz join together to form a point, a terminated crystal is born. When both ends of a crystal join in this fashion, Double Terminated Crystals are created. These specialized crystals have the capacity to draw in as well as emanate out energy from either end of the crystal. By uniting the energies together in the central body of the crystal, a Double Terminated Crystal can then project that unified essence out from both ends. This blending of forces allows the Double Terminated Crystal to be used in special meditations and advanced telepathic practices.

These crystals are complete unto themselves. They have reached a terminated peak of perfection on both ends. Instead of growing out of a hard rock surface in which single terminations are formed, Double Terminated Crystals grow in the center of softer clay. They know no limits or boundaries and have grown to completion on each of their polar ends. Double Terminated Crystals teach us that it is possible to be balanced in our dual expression of spirit and matter. They symbolize integration of both worlds into one single form, and show us that all polarities meet in the center. Double Terminated Crystals exude a sense of personal unity and are ideal to use with people who are mentally or emotionally unbalanced. By simply holding a Double Terminated Crystal in each hand for even five minutes, it will calm and relax one into a state of greater mental and emotional stability.

When negative energy has been blocked into the tissues, organs or aura of the body, Double Terminated Crystals can be placed on top of or held above the affected areas. This will create an energy vortex that will clear and dissolve any stagnant or unuseful energy. Double Terminated Crystals can be used on the head centers (such as the third eye or top of the crown) to expand the consciousness and harmoniously blend the logical with the intuitive and the physical with the spiritual. They can also be held directly onto different areas of the brain to stimulate underdeveloped aspects of the personality or consciousness. This type of treatment may evolve into futuristic crystal-laser brain surgery. Working with Double Terminated Crystals in this way can break up stubborn mental blockages which create addictive behaviors and unhealthy attitudes. As these old programs are erased, it is then possible to consciously recreate a positive perspective on the world and on one's life.

Double Terminated Crystals can be held over the chakra points and rotated in a clockwise direction to clear and open these centers. If possible, a Double Terminated Amethyst would be used over the third eye, a Double Terminated Citrine over the navel and a Double Terminated Smoky Quartz over the base chakra. Double Terminated Crystals are ideal to place in between the chakras during crystal healing layouts to integrate and harmonize the energy centers. They help to dissolve any blockage that may prevent the proper flow of energy through the body. Double Terminated crystals are also wonderful to use on points under the eyes and on the face where stress lines appear. This type of New Age facelift can reverse the aging process as it releases the stress that creates it and rejuvenates the sensitive tissues of the face.

Refining Telepathy

Another fascinating use of Double Terminated Crystals is for sharpening and refining telepathic powers. Working with a partner with whom you harmonize well, Double Terminated Crystals can be used to link together individual minds and thoughts, creating a stronger connection with the universal mind. Meditation exercises such as this should always follow positive affirmations to surround yourself with a protective white light. To practice these mental exercises, decide who will first receive the thoughts and who will project them. Each person will hold a Double Terminated Crystal. Sit cross-legged, with the spine straight, directly across from one another. The thought sender will hold the crystal in his/her right hand and place one of the terminated ends at his/her third eye center, with the other termination directed towards the partner's third eye. The receiver holds the Double Terminated Crystal in the left hand, terminations in the same position as sender. The receiver then becomes very still, open and sensitive to the thoughts being concentrated, visualized and projected by the sending party. Start by first concentrating and sending an image of a color, then a number, and advance into sending very specific thoughts and personal messages. Each party should practice being the giver as well as the receiver to develop both the passive and aggressive aspects of psychic communication. With regular practice, this meditation can develop a strong telepathic link between two people which will enable them to communicate even when they are miles apart. Double Terminated Crystals can also be used in personal prayers and meditations to send out thoughts of peace or to positively affirm personal goals.

Large Generator Crystals

Large Generator Crystals are instruments of great power and need to be used with knowledge and caution. If a Large Generator Crystal is set up properly, it becomes as a beacon of light that focuses and projects a high powered laser that can open the ethers to the material plane. Caution must be taken when working with these crystals. It is very important to project only the most positive humanitarian thoughts into them, for they magnify and intensify thoughts up to 1,000 times. This is why the Large Generator Crystals are ideal to use in group meditations and prayer circles for world peace. Using large generators in this way is one of the most powerful techniques for creating world change. The planetary aura is extremely sensitive to and affected by our thoughts and projections. These mental forms create the physical reality that we live in. If we can fill the atmosphere of the earth with thoughts of peace and love, the earth will have no choice but to manifest those thoughts into the lives and hearts of people everywhere. Large Generator Crystals are a priceless gift given to this planet as a tool for planetary transformation. If these power pieces are ever misused for egocentric or selfish purposes, the karmic ramifications could be extremely detrimental to the abuser. Use them wisely.

Large Generator Crystals are few in number. Some are as large as four feet and perfectly clear. Others are smaller (six to 36 inches), all with their own personality and presence. These generator crystals can be used in personal meditation practices or in crystal healings to set positive affirmations (see Chapter II, Group Healing Meditation). Large Generator Crystals should be upright, termination to the sky, when being used in healings or meditations. Sometimes a wooden stand can be custom-made to assist the crystal's horizontal position. When working with Large Generator Crystals, smaller Clear Quartz (two to six inches) generator crystals can be held up to the heart or to the third eye (terminations out, directed towards the large generator) to project thoughts, prayers or positive affirmations into the large crystal. As the large generator receives these psychic impressions that it is so susceptible to, it will amplify those thoughts and direct their intentions into the etheric plane. With the large generator's laser ray penetrating into the more subtle mental realm, existing patterns can be altered. This in turn will manifest in the physical world. For example, if someone is trying to quit smoking cigarettes, the thought and visualization of being completely free from the addiction could be projected into a large generator. The crystal will seed that impression deep into the mental plane which, if nurtured, will sprout into the desired reality.

When working with Large Generator Crystals, the ethers are very open and great power accessible. These crystals serve as an open two-way communication circuit, sending projections out as well as receiving and grounding higher energies onto the earth. To receive information or knowledge from the crystal and the more subtle realms, terminations of smaller Generator Crystals held in the hand are directed towards the third eye. These impressions are subtle and the mind may need to be trained to perceive and interpret them.

Large Generator Crystals can serve a multifold purpose. They can be used in many ways. They can direct telepathic messages, clear the atmosphere of negative energies, charge the aura, or be used in special white tantric practices between two people of like-mindedness. To practice this type of specialized meditation, sit across from your partner with your palms pressed together and the Large Generator Crystal upright between you. As you sit with eyes closed, breathe very deeply and focus on the energy that is building between you. The Large Generator Crystal will increase the force field of each party and merge those energies together. This meditation should only be practiced when two people choose to unite themselves on physical, mental, and spiritual levels. This meditation can be practiced every day, but should not exceed 11 minutes during each sitting. Working with a Large Generator Crystal in this way will strengthen the nervous system, allowing it to carry a greater electrical voltage along all of the nerve pathways in the body. This enables one to carry greater amounts of light force within the physical structures. It also purifies and strengthens the aura. These effects can also be gained when practicing a similar meditation alone. To do so, sit directly in front of the Large Generator Crystal and place your hands directly on the sides of the crystal. Breathe long and deep as you open yourself to the essence of the crystal and make yourself very receptive to its light. Again, do not exceed 11 minutes and if you feel light-headed or dizzy, release your hold on the crystal, move away from it, bring your forehead to the ground and breathe deeply. These particular meditations direct the crystal's light and energy into your own electrical magnetic field. A powerful vortex of energy spirals down into the Generator and radiates out to be received by the meditator. That light is then diffused into the multi colors of the spectrum, which in turn directly affect the central spinal column as they purify, stimulate and balance all of ths chakras. When working with this type of powerful energy source it is important to be physically, mentally and emotionally balanced. The above meditations will vibrate the nuclei of the atoms comprising the physical body, and in so doing purify the material vehicle to be able to contain greater and greater amounts of pure light.

Please use these crystals with respect and the utmost discrimination, and do not expose their energies to people that may not know how to use them.

Tabular Crystals

The Tabular is a very high vibration crystal, rarely recognized for the power that is instilled within it. Tabulars have a different energy frequency than any other quartz configuration. To date, their full potential has not been properly acknowledged or utilized. Tabular quartz are not found in all crystal mines and tend to be a rare specialty worth celebrating when discovered. Tabbies are very strong and powerful crystals. To simply describe, Tabulars are flat quartz crystals, with two of the opposing six sides being larger and wider. Often they will be double terminated and on special occasions live together in clusters.

The New Age Stones

Tabular Crystals serve as a bridge or connecting link between any two points. Their power lies in their ability to transmit from one side to the other while maintaining a perfect balance. Tabbies are a connecting communicator that will always strive to equalize energies by uniting the poles with a common base. They are excellent to use in balancing energies between two people, two chakras, or any two elements. When used in crystal healing layouts they can be placed between two chakra points to establish a link and integrate the energies. For example, a Tab could be placed in between the heart and throat center to allow for greater verbal expression of love. One could be placed between the heart and the solar plexus to balance the higher and lower bodies and release negative emotions. Tabulars can be directed into brain centers on the head to balance the hemispheres of the brain and align the intellect with the intuition. Tabs can be held in the hands or placed in between two people who choose to align and harmonize their energies. They are wonderful marriage counselors, as they help to bridge any gaps in communication or sharing. Double terminated Tabs can be programmed and used in telepathic communication between any two people of like mindedness. One person would program the crystal and the other would retrieve the information by psychically attuning to the crystal. This advanced form of correspondence may evolve to be one of the New Age methods of communication.

In cases of emotional hysteria or extreme mental anguish, a Tabular Crystal can be held in each hand to balance the energy flows in the body and assist the person to establish communication with his/her higher self. Results can be noticed almost immediately as a healing occurs on a mental level that will allow the link between the soul force and the personality to take place. Tabbies do not break old mental patterns; instead they serve as the bridge between the higher and lower, the outer and the inner selves. Tabbies are good to keep in a first aid kit or to carry with you to be used in case of emergencies.

In advanced meditations, Tabular Crystals can be used to establish conscious communication with discarnate entities, extra-terrestrial beings, or personal past life connections. This soul level communication requires a calm stillness of mind and a personal affinity and relationship with the Tabular Crystal being used. These meditations require a trained mind and should not be attempted if under the influence of any external substance (drugs or alcohol). To practice this meditation, attune yourself to the crystal by holding it in your left hand and placing it against each chakra point for several minutes, establishing a link between all of your energy centers and the Tab. Finally, leave the crystal to rest at the top of your head as you concentrate on that area. Visualize a vortex of energy spiraling down through the crown chakra and allow it to come to rest at the third eye. Perceive with your sixth sense and allow the inner mind to interpret the symbols, images, impressions or messages that you receive. Trust without a doubt the lessons you attain while practicing such meditations and strive to integrate this new information into your daily life.

Tabular crystals often times become personal meditation pieces or private teacher crystals because they establish such a strong link between you and your higher self. They will attract themselves towards the people who can best attune to their frequency and benefit from their power. Tabular Crystals will usually appear on the scene at crucial stages of development when you are advancing to the next step or level of awareness and need a friend to help bridge the gap and assist in crossing the threshold.

The Record Keeper

The Record Keeper is one of the most sacred crystals that could ever be witnessed or worked with. Eons of wisdom can be stored within such crystals, and when properly attuned to, can reveal ancient knowledge and profound secrets of the Universe. These crystals have been consciously and purposely programmed by either the oversoul beings who created the vibrational frequencies that would allow human life to evolve on earth, or by their direct lineage—the Atlantians and the Lemurians. These were the pure races that first inhabited our earth. This advanced race of beings came from far beyond our solar system, and as they traveled and evolved, they stored within their memory patterns all of the lessons and experiences from worlds and universes beyond. When they came to our earth they seeded the first root race, which has now come of age and is reaching the crest of evolution when this invaluable knowledge can be received. These enlightened beings wished to preserve the secrets of the universe so that when the human soul became ready it could inherit a fortune of cosmic knowledge. Special crystals were chosen. These were programmed with galaxies of information and placed deep within the earth. At the exact right time they would come to the surface of the planet to be used by the exact right person. It is also believed that some of the Record Keeper Crystals simply materialize out of thin air when the time has come to share their stories. When this information is tapped into, worlds of experience and learning can be embraced by the human soul.

The purpose of accessing information from Record Keeper Crystals is two-fold. First, to satisfy the thirst that each soul has for the truth and for knowledge concerning the origin of the human race and the origin of the human soul. Secondly, as individuals come to know this truth within themselves and feel connected to their source, planetary humanitarian goals can be met as each person becomes a healing agent to the earth.

Record Keeper Crystals have their own security system. Only the pure in heart can attune their consciousness to receive the libraries of wisdom contained within. Souls of high vibration are now given the opportunity to seek this eternal knowledge and engrain it into their beings. It is not information to be given freely, it is rather an enhancement to one's own light, a deeper access to personal wisdom and greater peace to be used in your world. It is not a healing energy. It is wisdom.

Record Keepers all have a sacred symbol engraved on one of their facets. These symbols are not easily seen and usually need to be searched out by looking at the crystal in a bright light while closely examining all the faces and facets. If a crystal is a Record Keeper, a small perfect triangle will be found on one of the six faces forming the termination. These small triangles are not the facets themselves. They have actually been etched into the crystals. If you run your finger over the triangle you will feel the indentation. This ancient universal trinity symbol represents the perfect balance achieved when the physical, mental, and emotional aspects of our being are aligned with a point of spiritual light at the top. It is also the symbol of the all-seeing third eye. The triangle is the eye. The triangle is the eye of the crystal and serves as a doorway into powerful wisdom. This symbol on the Record Keeper Crystal indicates vast resources beneath its surface that are capable of being psychically retrieved.

The Atlantian civilization fell because cosmic power and universal knowledge were being abused and misused for selfish purposes. Many of the Atlantians who retained their wisdom programmed Record Keepers to retrieve in future lifetimes. Much of this sacred knowledge has been inaccessible until now. It is of vital importance to accept full responsibility and have complete respect and reverence for this information. If these crystals, or the knowledge contained within them, is ever misused again, damage could occur that would make this information inaccessible to this planet.

It is a responsibility to work with a Record Keeper. The information received may be unlike anything you have witnessed or experienced. Data may be stored in them that has absolutely nothing to do with physical life on planet earth. The person receiving the information must not only train their mind to be open to receive inconceivable concepts, but also must be capable of processing the information somehow into their lives. With advanced training these crystals can transport the consciousness into higher dimensions and greater realities. The purpose of such experiences and of receiving such phenomenal information is not to escape from the world here on earth, but rather to incorporate higher knowledge, wisdom, peace and love onto our planet. As the human mind expands to encompass a greater and higher truth about life and the universe, the entire planet will evolve into the Aquarian Age.

Generally speaking, Record Keeper Crystals are personal meditation crystals and are sometimes not even touched or seen by others. To meditate with a Record Keeper, place the small triangle directly upon your third eye center, close your eyes, still the mind, relax and receive. If you are meant to experience a Record Keeper, one will attract itself to you. You may already have one in your collection. Check to see if the white inclusions inside of the crystal resemble spiraling galaxies, and see if any of the facets that form the termination have a triangle engraved on it. The type of crystal that is most receptive to be programmed as a Record Keeper is clear Quartz Single Generator Crystals. On occasion they can also be found on crystals comprising clusters or on Amethysts, Citrine or Smoky Quartz.

Teacher Crystals

Teacher Crystals are complete unto themselves, containing within them vast resources of personal and universal knowledge. They are here to teach and virtually have nothing to learn from us humans. These crystals are completely unique and look like no others. Each Teacher Crystal is its own multi-dimensional universe. Sometimes they are double terminated Tabular Clusters, or perfectly clear Large Generators. They can be any combination or variety of form that quartz manifests in. You will know them by their presence and authority. They have a regal essence that warrants immediate respect.

In the 12 years that I have been working with crystals, I have only recognized three of these magnificent teachers. To my knowledge, these crystals are for certain specific individuals. When those special people are drawn to one of these crystals, they will immediately know that it is for their use and that it has information contained within it that is necessary for their next step in evolution. Although many will be drawn to the beauty and power of Teacher Crystals, they will actually be worked with by only a very few. Once a Teacher Crystal has completed transmitting its wisdom to one student, it will move on. It is then the responsibility of the graduating student to release it to the next person that claims its presence.

The ways in which Teacher Crystals are worked with are very personalized. The Teacher Crystals will communicate to the student the exact way they are to be used. Some are placed under the pillow or put on a night stand while sleeping to assist one in their out-of-the-body experiences. Some Teacher Crystals record dreams and lessons of the night to be retrieved in the morning. In this way the crystal helps integrate different levels of consciousness. Some Teacher Crystals are used in meditation to initiate Kundalini experiences and some are to be worn at all times. In whatever way they are means to be used, they will work directly with the individual's process and assist them in taking the next step. Teacher Crystals are valuable friends and extremely trustworthy, for they are totally attuned to you and concerned with your fulfillment.

Teacher Crystals will appear in your life if it is destined. If they do, enjoy their presence, attune your mind to communicate with them, learn their invaluable lessons, love them, and then give them the freedom to continue their work with another person. It may be years that you have one, it may even be a lifetime. But if your lessons have been completed and if someone else arrives on the scene and knows that the crystal is their teacher, you must release it. Teacher Crystals are a most precious gift, whose final lessons are detachment and sharing.

Rainbow Crystals

As pure white light diffuses and expresses its multidimensional prismatic colors, the rainbow is given birth to. Each one of the rainbow colors manifests its own unique ray of light with its individual essence, vibration, presence and purpose. Rainbows are the closest manifestations of pure white light that can be witnessed on the physical plane. Rainbows are the second phase of pure light developing into denser forms. As light enters the physical plane, it expresses itself in an infinite number of ways. In reality, everything is the play of that light and color upon itself. Rainbows are a most special symbol of the light in panoramic color and multi-faceted forms. They are representative of the entire creation. When rainbows are seen after rainstorms, it is a reminder of hope and renewed life. The rainbow unites and integrates the heavens with the earth, and upon that ray life can be born anew. The rainbow is a sign that the sun is always behind the clouds of our doubt and confusion.

On special occasions these brilliant representatives of the light can be found in Clear Quartz Crystals. These rainbows have chosen to live within the inner sanctum of the crystal's world. Quartz Crystals have the remarkable capacity to capture the rainbow ray and display its glory and magic to us. These special Rainbow Crystals are a gift from the universe to whoever is blessed to receive one.

The New Age Stones

The rainbows found in crystals dance delightfully as the crystals are turned and played with in the light. Rainbow Crystals can teach us how to be multifaceted in our own unique expression of light while still remaining pure and colorfully conscious in all aspects of living.

Rainbow Crystals can be used in meditation to escort the consciousness into the realm of pure color. In Rainbow Crystal meditations, the human awareness can travel the rainbow ray all the way back to the source of pure light, the great central sun. This eternal source of light is the foundation upon which all reality is built. Catching even a glimpse, or experiencing this omnipotent essence even for an instant, is enough to transform the very nature of one's life. When this universal connection is plugged into, there is nothing that cannot be accomplished or transformed. When the human soul aligns with this cosmic force, reality takes on a new dimension and one becomes personally empowered. To practice Rainbow Crystal meditations, either hold the crystal to eye level and gaze into the rainbow and allow your consciousness to perceive the true nature of light and color, or close the eyes and place the crystal to the third eye and allow its essence to take you on an inner journey.

Rainbow Crystals are wonderful to use in crystal healings for people who are experiencing sadness, grief or depression. By simply holding the Rainbow Crystal in the left hand and placing it against the heart chakra, those feelings will be dissolved and neutralized to be replaced with joy, enthusiasm, confidence and love. As the rainbow ray beams its multicolored magic into our lives we can better serve the forces of light and love. Use these delightful gifts with pleasure and in joy.

Programmed Projector Crystals

Projector Crystals can be various different types of Quartz. Sometimes they are Large Single Generators with a flat base that they stand on. Sometimes clusters are used or crystals that only have two terminated points but share a common flat base. The prerequisite that must be met to qualify as a Projector Crystal is that the base be flat (and preferably clear), and that the terminations of the crystal be directed and pointing out in the *same* direction. This will enable the crystal to beam its projection out in a very focused and concentrated manner. Projector Crystals are ideal to use in programming because they can send out thoughts and images that are transferred into them.

To program these crystals, bring the termination of the crystal to the third eye center and concentrate an image, thought or prayer into the crystal. The crystal will receive these subtle mental impressions and project them out into the environment to assist in creating the desired results. These projections can be healing energy sent out for other people, positive affirmations, desired goals, or planetary prayers. Whatever the projection, see it very clearly in your mind's eye and then beam that thought out into the receptive base of the crystal. When sending healing energy to other people, a picture of that person may be placed under the crystal to amplify its effect. If you are affirming personal goals, you may wish to write a short summary and place the paper underneath the crystal. If sending light out for the planet, a small picture of the world could be set up next to the Projector Crystal to intensify its effects. By programming crystals in this way, those positive conscious thoughts continue to be emanated out through the crystal throughout the day and night when your attention has to be elsewhere. By keeping a constant thought projection occurring, the desired result will have a much greater chance of manifesting in a shorter length of time. These Programmed Crystals will carry those thought impressions until they are cleansed. To clear the former programming and prepare the crystal for a new thought projection, the water-sun method of cleansing is best to use.

It is also possible to program crystals in this manner to create a desired atmosphere or before giving them as gifts. For example, if a very special friend is coming to visit, a Projector Crystal could be programmed with images of that person thoroughly enjoying him/herself, relaxing and being filled wih positive energy. A crystal could also be programmed with similar thoughts and given as a gift to continue and strengthen the friendship after the visit. It is also nice to give Programmed Crystals to people who are in hospitals or bed-ridden. Send your healing energy into the crystal and when you give it, make sure that the terminations are pointing directly towards the person who is to receive the energy. These subtle projections that are programmed into the crystals will fill the environment with positive thoughts and healing energy and will create a definite effect, irregardless of whether or not people are able to understand it consciously. The seeds will be planted in the subconscious mind and at the right time will sprout and blossom.

Crystals can also be programmed with your presence and placed in environments in which you would like to be a part of and maintain connection. If a friend is going to a special place where you are unable to go, you can project your essence into a crystal and have them take it along on the trip. In this way, a part of your presence will accompany them. By leaving these crystals in special places on the planet (the pyramids, temples, sacred mountains, etc.), it is possible to set up a psychic connection with power points on the earth and draw upon their uplifting energies.

Crystal Balls

Pure Quartz Crystal Balls possess power that one must attune with and train to use. The Crystal Ball has always been a symbol of the occult, of hidden wisdom and fortune telling. Crystal Balls are objects of authority which can have great influence in the development of psychic abilities. When Crystal Balls are gazed into, it is possible to see into the past or tune into the future. This is why Crystal Balls have been used as a tool in prediction for thousands of years. When psychics use Crystal Balls in their readings, what they are doing is seeing an image of the person's aura reflected into the ball. Being able to interpret those images, it is possible to "see" and know many things about a person.

To practice this type of mental exercise and develop this ability, sit directly across from a partner with a Crystal Ball between the two of you. Gaze with half closed eyes into the ball and allow the mind to become concentrated and stilled. As the inner vision of the third eye is opened, energy patterns can be seen reflected in the ball. These patterns will become clear and focused as the mind is trained. Immediately trust what is being seen and do not hesitate to spontaneously express it. As this flow of intuitive expression continues, it is possible to become so attuned to the Crystal Ball that the impressions seen within it are as clear and defined as the ball itself. Developing the art of crystal gazing is one way to open the all-seeing third eye and see beyond the illusion of time and space.

Pure Quartz Crystal Balls are usually expensive but well worth the price if they are put to use. Their presence during crystal healings assists the healer to become more in tune with the person being healed. Most Crystal Balls are not completely clear, displaying swirls of galaxies, whispy clouds or even rainbows within them. Each ball has its own individual personality and presence to share. Some Crystal Balls are perfectly clear and transparent. These are best to use in personal meditations to gain greater spiritual clarity and insight. To pratice this type of meditation, hold the Crystal Ball in the palms of both hands at either the heart or third eye center. Gaze into the ball for three minutes and allow the image of clear white light to be engrained into the consciousness. Continue in this fashion for up to 30 minutes, refocusing the awareness from the external ball of light to the internal experience of that light.

Crystal Balls are priceless powerful objects, and as with all use of such pieces, they should always be used with knowledge and the best of intentions.

Phantom Crystals

On rare occasions, when looking into the inner world of a crystal, smaller pyramid shaped inclusions are found inside. These internal mirrors of the crystal are called Phantoms and are much like the rings inside a tree, in that they mark the growth pattern that the crystal has undergone in its evolution. Phantom Crystals have experienced many lifetimes of learning while embodying the same physical form. The phantoms inside have recorded a period of growth where the crystal came to a completion, stopped growing and then continued on, beyond the expected and into the unknown. Some Phantom Crystals have many internal graduating lines that when attuned to can reveal the secrets of the inner life of the crystal.

Phantom Crystals are rare and intriguing. They represent the multi-phases of development that can be experienced in one lifetime. Phantom Crystals are a culmination of knowledge that was gained by the crystal in its own unique evolutionary cycles. It is possible to use these precious tools in meditation to learn to travel deep within the records of your own soul. By staring deep within the phantom inside the crystal, and then closing your eyes and taking that image into your own inner mind, it is possible to travel along your own memories and trace the geneology of your soul back to its source. The power of such an experience cannot be overstated. It is a journey that one embarks upon after years, if not lifetimes, of purification and preparation. Phantom Crystals can be powerful tools in this prepatory process. Their symbolic presence provides clues to the multi-faceted lives that we all live and can reveal to the purified mind the truth of manifold existence.

If used properly, Phantom Crystals can unlock and open the doors to the sacred sanctums of the soul. They are the key-holders to the higher dimensions and the inner planes. Use them with great respect and humility and they will teach you more about yourself than you ever knew. Phantom Crystal meditations require mental discipline and patience. It is important to remember when practicing these meditations that the normal waking mind is not accustomed to perceiving the subtle vibrations that these crystals emanate. It will take time to train the mind to be still enough to interpret these impressions. But with perseverance and practice the Phantom Crystal will become a most valuable and important teacher to the sincere student.

Light Box Crystals

Light boxes are rectangular or square wooded structures with a hole in the center for a small light bulb to be placed. Color filters or jells are placed over the hole where the light shines up through the box. Light Box Crystals are placed over the filters. When crystals are used in this way they intensify and project those color rays into the environment to be used for healing and upliftment. For example, if you want to bring in healing energy while you were practicing a crystal layout, a green filter could be used and a crystal placed with the termination directed towards you. To create a peaceful meditative atmosphere, a blue filter could be used with a cluster placed on top to disseminate the calming blue ray. When crystals are used in this way they become intensifiers and magnifiers of specific color frequencies, which in turn create specific moods or effects. When light and color are reflected through crystals in this way, the inner worlds and dimension of the crystals come to life and can be witnessed and appreciated.

Light Box Crystals can be either flat based, Single Generator Crystals or clusters. The only requirement to be accepted as a Light Box Crystal is the capability of reflecting light from the base up through the entire crystal. Crystals with dense rock bases are unable to perform this function. Light Box Crystals usually have crystalline bases and are often double-teminated or naturally terminated on the bottom.

After a crystal has been used on a light box with a particular color and you wish to use it with another color, it is best to cleanse the crystal first (water-sun method is sufficient). Light Box Crystals are usually Clear Quartz but other crystals, such as Fluorite Pyramids, can also be used and experimented with (see Fluorite Pyramid).

AMETHYST

Amethyst reflects the purple ray, one of the colors for the third eye center. It is the color that can be seen on special evening sunsets, as dusk transforms daylight into darkness. It is the color that symbolizes the change of consciousness from the normal waking state into the twilight regions of altered awareness. In those most enchanted moments of shifting energies the Amethyst ray reflects the essence of magic and the ability to transform from one reality to another.

Amethyst is one of the best stones to use for meditation. Since the Amethyst color is the highest vibration of the third eye, an Amethyst stone can be placed directly over this area (while a person is lying face up) to usher in a meditative state. Amethyst's gentle persuasion temporarily stills the mundane thought processes that usually inundate the consciousness so that the mind can experience tranquility. Amethyst guides the awareness away from self-centered thought patterns as it lures the mind towards a deeper understanding. As the mind surrenders and thoughts subside, glimmers and hints of a greater knowing filter into the consciousness. Amethyst energy shows the mind how to be humble so that the door to the higher mind can be opened. The inner calm and peace initiated by this stone enable one to dive deep into the ocean of silence and participate in the serenity that exists beyond constant mental activity.

Amethyst is here to teach the lesson of humility. It is willing to show the mind how to surrender at the altar of the self. Only then can one cross the threshold into the realm of true knowing and wisdom. Only when the mind realizes that there is something greater than itself, that there are limitations to its conceptions, and that the senses can perceive only a small portion of the total truth, can it begin to grasp the meaning of life and existence. Only by letting go of all that was believed to be real can the ultimate reality be known. Only by bowing can the circulation rush into the head to give the experience of higher consciousness. Amethyst is here to say "Let go and trust"; "Give it all up so that you may receive more"; "Surrender, that you may see beyond the cycles and circumstances that consume your attention and attach your consciousness to the physical world"; "Bow, that you may become part of a much greater whole"; "Become empty, that you may be filled completely"; "Humble yourself, that the powers of the universe can direct and guide your course."

Because Amethyst initiates wisdom and greater understanding, it is very useful for people who are grieving over the loss of a loved one. Its presence lends comfort as it subliminally communicates that there is no death, only transitioning and the changing of forms. Amethyst will silently counsel, saying "Celebrate the freedom your loved one has found; rejoice that the soul has been freed from the confinement of the physical body; assist the process by releasing your sorrow and instead send thoughts of joy and prayers of love." Death is mourned only because we have not been educated as to the eternal existence of the soul. Amethyst could be called "the soul stone" as it sends its message to that level of being. It initiates deep soul experiences. Because Amethyst communicates directly to the soul, it is an ideal stone to hold or meditate upon during the death experience. When strong identification with the soul force is made, the release of the temporal physical body is accomplished more easily and the death transition can then be made with assurity and peace. It is therefore an ideal stone to give to people with terminal illnesses or to use in preparation for a conscious death experience.

Because of the calming mental effect, Amethyst is a stone that can be used for overworked, overstressed, or overwhelmed mental states. It is one of the best stones to use for tension or migraine headaches as it eases the mental anxieties that tend to cause such conditions. Amethyst purple is comprised of hues of blue and red. The blue color brings peace to the red-action energy. It is therefore good for people who tend to be hot-headed and easily angered (red energies). It can be held, worn, or meditated upon when the temper rises to restore mental equilibrium. Amethyst is especially helpful for people suffering from recurrent nightmares. Before retiring, hold an Amethyst crystal up to the forehead and program it to guide the mind safely through the sleep state. Then place it under the pillow and sleep securely. Amethyst can be placed under the pillow during sleep by anyone wishing to inspire sweet dreams.

Single Amethyst crystals or small clusters can be held in the left hand (termination towards the arm) during meditation to draw Amethyst energy into the body. This will relax the physical system and make one more vulnerable and sensitive to meditative experiences. Large clusters of Amethyst are ideal to place on meditation altars and use as concentration objects to gaze upon. This type of meditation will train the mind to be centered and calm while the awareness is focused on the objective world.

Amethyst is very good friends with Rose Quartz. While the gentle purple of Amethyst calms the mind, the soft pink of Rose Quartz soothes the heart. These stones can be used together in crystal healings, worn as jewelry, or meditated upon to bring about a peaceful balance of mental and emotional energies.

Fortunately, Amethyst crystals are abundant and easy to find. Because they are one of the most beautiful crystal forms, they are occasionally found in variety stores as well as most rock shops. They range in color from deep dark purple to almost clear white with only a purple hue. Generally speaking, the clearer and the darker, the more valuable and expensive. Dark gem quality Amethysts are usually cut and faceted and rank in quality, beauty and price with other precious gems. These stones are best set in gold and worn as jewelry to display their beauty and to receive their special effects. Amethyst clusters, Single Generators and geodes are wonderful and vital additions to a crystal healing collection. Small Amethyst clusters are usually placed on the third eye area during crystal healings. Single Generator Crystals can be used to trace the meridians to balance subtle energy flows. Small single crystals can be set and worn with the termination pointing down to direct the flow of Amethyst energy into the body.

ROSE QUARTZ

Rose Quartz is the corner-stone for the heart chakra. Its energy is essential to self-fulfillment and inner peace. The soft soothing pink of Rose Quartz comforts and heals any wounds the heart has accumulated. It is a stone for those who are unable to experience the joy of living because they never had love given to them. It is for people who have not experienced the true essence of love and are therefore unable to access the inner realms of the heart. Being an important member of the Quartz family, Rose Quartz inherits dynamic intensity and healing power. In addition, it manifests a calm vibration of soft sweet pink.

Often when children are reared they do not receive the love and nurturing that is vitally necessary in the development of a positive self image. If the basic emotional needs are not met, a child will subconsciously conclude that he/she is not worth loving and as a result will not know how to love him/herself or how to give and share love with others. Children suffering from this type of deprivation grow up with attitudes about themselves and about life that perpetuate their feelings of loneliness and worthlessness. Not feeling good about oneself, it is very difficult to attract positive circumstances and fulfilling relationships. Unfortunately, adults who never received love as children will often be unable to provide it to their children, and the vicious cycle will continue.

Unless a deep inner healing takes place and these primal imprints are erased, there is little chance for inner peace or true happiness. Rose Quartz is the healer for such internal wounds. It teaches one the power of forgiveness and reprograms the heart to love itself. Rose Quartz teaches that the source of love comes from within the self and from that source of infinite love any wound, no matter how deep or painful, can be healed. Rose Quartz, upon healing the heart, will also show that the lesson contained in many negative childhood experiences is for the self to learn how to love and nurture itself.

Rose Quartz gently penetrates into the inner chambers of the heart chakra, where all emotional experiences are recorded and stored. As Rose Quartz witnesses the trauma written therein it empathizes, understands and begins to dissolve the accumulated burdens that suppress the heart's ability to give and receive love. Rose Quartz is like a wise old woman that knows all of the answers and can heal with a mere glance. As the Rose Quartz energy is sensed, the soul sighs with relief as it intuitively knows that at last the healing has come. This divine Rose Quartz essence begins to circulate energy throughout the heart chakra, bringing inner nourishment and comfort. As the presence of love is felt, the sorrows, fears and resentments that have constricted the flow of love are replaced with a deep sense of personal fulfillment. This forms the foundation upon which inner peace and contentment become a personal reality.

This Rose Quartz healing process may take many months or even years to accomplish, depending upon the depth of internalized pain and the personal willingness to reprogram the heart. As the process unfolds, be prepared to recall many past forgotten experiences that initially created the emotional stress. Allow the tears to flow as you encourage the release of suppressed feelings. During these vulnerable times always carry a piece of Rose Quartz with you or wear Rose Quartz jewelry. This is a time when much of your energies will be internalized and devoted to your own healing process. Try to plan quiet peaceful time for yourself and be with people who are understanding and aware of the healing crisis that is taking place. These times are ideal to practice the power of positive affirmation as you convince yourself how much you love yourself. Look at yourself in the mirror, as you stand naked before it, and tell yourself how beautiful you are. Look yourself in the eyes and express your appreciation for all that you have been through. Reprogram yourself as you listen to what you have to say and communicate to yourself your deepest heart-felt secrets. Consciously fill in all of the vacant spaces and learn to trust yourself—that no matter what happens, you will always be there for you! This type of self love is the only real basis for security. All other attachments in life are destined to change and it is only the self, united with itself that forms the foundation upon which all of life's changes can be effectively and maturely adjusted to.

If you are treating others with crystal healings and wish to use Rose Quartz on the heart chakra, be prepared for emotional releases and the surfacing of suppressed and often forgotten memories and feelings. In the days following the crystal healing, be on call to comfort, counsel and listen, as this is one of the extracurricular activities that Rose Quartz requests. When using Rose Quartz in crystal healings it is best to use at least three stones. Place one directly over the heart chakra point (in the center of the chest in direct line with the nipples) and one both above and below it. If you have two more pieces, place them on either side of the center one, creating a cross formation on the chest. Kunzite and Pink Tourmaline are also heart chakra stones (see their specific purposes) and can be used in conjunction with the internal healing powers of Rose Quartz. It is of added benefit to place an Amethyst crystal on the forehead and a Citrine on the navel to balance the mental and physical energies as Rose Quartz performs emotional surgery upon the heart. Inform your client that after a Rose Quartz crystal healing they will probably be extra sensitive, vulnerable and emotional. Advise them to take extra good care and treat themselves to nice things for at least 24 hours. Rose Quartz can also be used in chakra balance layouts, as a center piece in a heart chakra charge, or in any general layout (see Chapter III).

As the heart is nourished and healed from the Rose Quartz essence it becomes fertile ground for the flowers of love to grow. As the gentle pink ray is implanted and infused in the aura, blossoms of contentment unfold and the true meaning of love can be known. Only after first learning to give love to the self is it possible to truly love others. Unless one is fulfilled from within they will always have expectations and disappointments from the love they receive from others. But if the heart is complete unto itself, then the love that is shared with others will be pure and have no expectations attached to it. When the eternal well-spring of the heart has been tapped, the very act of giving replenishes the love and sharing becomes the reward. When one learns how to truly love on this level their very presence is healing to those around them and their being radiates with light.

True love is the highest degree attained at the heart chakra and this process is initiated with Rose Quartz.

Rose Quartz comes in many forms. Most popular, easy to find and inexpensive are the small tumbled stones. These are ideal to use in crystal healing layouts or to carry in pockets or pouches. Cabachoned or faceted pieces are usually of a better quality and more expensive. They are also wonderful to use in layouts or can be set in gold and worn as jewelry. Rose Quartz jewelry is very popular these days and can be found in many different sizes of beads and unique shapes. Necklaces of Rose Quartz are ideal to wear because they are worn against the chest and stimulate many of the heart chakra points. Rose Quartz clusters are rare, hard to find and usually very expensive. Rarer still are the Single Generators. If located and affordable, Rose Quartz clusters or single points would be an asset to any crystal collection or an exceptional power piece to use in crystal healings.

CITRINE QUARTZ

Citrine Quartz reflects a color range from light gold to dark brown. This important member of the quartz family is specifically for the navel chakra. Its yellow ray stimulates activity in all of the physical systems. Citrine energy is like that of the sun; warming, comforting, penetrating, energizing and life giving.

The consciousness associated with the navel center is one of physical and material power. As we learn that abundance is our divine heritage, Citrine energy will be there to assist us in attracting to us the riches of the earth. When the navel chakra is evolved and refined, it is possible to attract whatever material wealth is needed to live as gods upon the earth. What actually happens in this state of consciousness is that one is so attuned to the creative light force that by simply clarifying, defining and projecting what is wanted, it will be drawn towards you like a powerful magnet. It is very important to only use this power of attracting and manifestation for the highest good. If used for selfish ego purposes, what is drawn will become attachments that will eventually bring loss and sorrow to the possessor. Citrine can be used to build the light force around and within the physical body so that the creative power can be directed and consciously used.

The navel chakra is the main center for physical manifestation. People whose consciousness is completely attached to earth plane materialism could be said to be "caught at their navel". Mastery of the navel center, which is one of the most powerful energy centers, will test the character and integrity of the individual. It is so easy to become attached to the pleasures and riches of the earth. But, in doing so, one loses sight of the source from which all wealth originates, and becomes engrossed in the illusion of the earth. Only when the navel center is ruled by the crown chakra can its energy be channeled properly and without fear of becoming captive to transitory pleasures.

One of the colors for the crown chakra is gold. This golden ray manifests in high quality Citrine colors which can be used to channel that pure crown energy into the navel to be used for conscious manifestation and creative purposes. The transmission of the golden ray into the body will serve to protect and direct the use of this powerful creative force in one's life. To direct this golden ray into the body during a crystal healing, place a gem quality faceted Citrine at the navel while a clear yellow-gold Citrine generator is held at the crown. Visualize a beam of gold light connecting the navel with the crown.

Because the navel is so closely associated with the solar plexus (which stores emotional memories), the navel's physical vitality can often be usurped by the solar vortex. Citrine clusters can be used at the heart chakra, solar plexus, and navel to help reenergize the body and align the navel center with the heart center. Often times constriction of the navel chakra will create various physical problems such as poor digestion, kidney and bladder infections and constipation. Citrine clusters can be placed directly over affected areas to break up and dissolve the psychic and emotional correlations that create the physical problems. For example, if someone is constipated and unable to properly digest and assimilate their food, chances are that they are also unable to adjust to external disturbances in their life. Citrine is the perfect stone to use to strengthen the psychic as well as the phsyical body. This added strength will enable one to better adjust to the numerous influences that affect the overall state of personal health. Citrine is for psychic digestion and assimilation. Its energy assists one to process life's events, put them in right order, and get rid of the waste. This ability allows one to flow with life instead of trying to hang onto it.

In cases where people are overly sensitive and extremely vulnerable to outside energies and influences, Citrine can be worn, carried, or used in crystal healings. The vibrant yellow orange color will increase the amount of light surrounding the body and in so doing, create a protective aura. This will make a person less susceptible to negative vibrations and influences. Citrine is also a good stone to have present in situations where one needs to feel confident and secure. It is a stone that speaks with assurance and will transfer that sense of inner security into your aura. It vibrates with the essence of the golden white light from the crown chakra so it makes that radiance a living reality in your life. High quality Citrine reflects the golden ray so clearly that it beams that positive sunlight energy directly into your environment. In single generator form, Citrine crystals can be set in gold and worn with the termination facing downwards. This way the crystals become powerful channelers of crown energy into the body. Citrine initiates a higher vibrational force wherever they are and however they are used.

Citrine is the best stone to use when trying to accomplish matters of earthly existence such as business, education, interpersonal relationships or family matters. Citrine's dynamic expression of refined use of spiritual power can be an aid to any life event or situation. By meditating upon Citrine, one feels a glowing warmth from within and from without. Citrine's sole purpose is to manifest the golden light force onto the physical plane. It does a very good job!

Citrine is available in clusters, single and double terminated generator crystals, gem quality cut and faceted stones and small tumbled rocks. For a reasonable price, the clear projection of the golden ray can be purchased and put to active use.

SMOKY QUARTZ

Smoky Quartz is one of the most brilliant of all the dark stones. It ranks first in ability to contain the highest amount of light force in a black color. Because the color black is associated with the first chakra, Smoky Quartz is one of the most powerful stones to use in crystal healing layouts to stimulate and purify this energy center. If unevolved, the consciousness associated with the root chakra can be very decadent and concerned only with personal gratification. But when this chakra becomes radiant with light and balanced with the upper chakras, it then becomes the foundation upon which the spiritual force is manifested in the physical body. Smoky Quartz channels the white light energy of the crown chakra into the first chakra to be rooted deep into the physical plane. As this occurs, one becomes personally empowered on earth with the forces and blessings of the heavens.

When wearing Smoky Quartz in jewelry or using it in crystal healing layouts, its energy will initiate movement of the primal forces in the body. It will activate the survival instincts of the first chakra, but in a purified form. It will give one the sense of pride about walking the earth and inhabiting a human body. Smoky Quartz inspires one to accept the challenge and responsibility to change the quality of one's personal life and life on earth. Smoky Quartz makes vivid the vision of heaven on earth and promises the rightful heritage that can be inherited by all creatures while dwelling upon this planet. The hope of joyful living is a potential reality that can be created if each individual claims the light as his own and sincerely strives to manifest that light in daily actions. Smoky quartz is a clear example of the ability to be filled with light while inhabiting a physical form.

Because of its grounding ability, Smoky Quartz is a very good stone to use with people that tend to be suicidal in nature or ambivalent about the world. By bringing more light force onto the material plane, escapist attitudes can be transformed into the incentive necessary to change one's life. Smoky quartz helps one come to terms with their body, their heart, their life and their world. This acceptance will allow one to feel more love for him/herself and others. Smoky Quartz draws the love force of the heart chakra into the root chakra to be grounded and utilized. It is therefore beneficial to use this stone with people who are depressed, fatigued, spaced-out, or who have high ideals and aspirations but are unable to live up to their own standards. Smoky Quartz gives one the power to manifest their dreams and visions of earth.

Unlike some stones that will surface suppressed negative patterns (such as Malachite), Smoky quartz tends to dissolve those energies as it encounters them. Smoky quartz has a high frequency light vibration that will dissipate and purify most negative patterns and auric debris. Working with Smoky quartz can create somewhat of a radical change in behavior as aspects of the lower egocentric nature are erased and replaced with positive attitudes and habit patterns.

The root chakra is associated with the anus and the ability to adequately dispose of waste products. Smoky Quartz is the stone to use to psychically as well as physically process the elements of life and release the unuseful byproducts. Smoky quartz enables one to assimilate more in life by teaching how to let go of what is no longer needed for growth. This freedom of nonattachment allows one to stay attuned to the light, instead of being consumed by life.

Unfortunately, a lot of the Smoky Quartz on the market today is not truly Smoky Quartz. Most of what is sold as Smoky Quartz is Clear Quartz that has been radiated to make it turn a dark color. With a little sensitivity it is easy to determine of a smoky crystal has been radiated. If they have, they are usually very dark and unnatural looking. When Quartz is artificially treated in this manner, it becomes very traumatized and will need to be cleansed and healed before using in crystal healings. The best way to neutralize the negative effects of radiation is to submerge the affected stone in sea salt for three days and then place it upon a Clear Quartz cluster (preferably under a pyramid structure) until you sense that the stone has recovered from its ordeal. It can then be used in healing but should be cleansed after each treatment.

True Smoky Quartz will be clear and transparent with varying degrees of dark tones. Of course, true Smoky Quartz is the best to use in all cases. It is possible to find beautiful natural Smoky Quartz in single generators and cluster form. Smoky Quartz clusters or single points can be placed at the instep of each foot, at the knees, and/or in each hand during crystal healing layouts. If the termination of the crystal is directed towards the body, the stones will channel and recirculate higher forces into the body. If the terminations are directed away from the body, the stones will direct negative energies out of the physical and subtle bodies. Smoky Quartz can also be cut and faceted into beautiful gem quality stones that can be worn as jewelry or placed upon the groin points during crystal healings. Single Generator Crystals can be used to direct the flow of energy from the crown chakra into the first chakra. This is done by holding a clear Single Generator Crystal at the crown chakra as you slowly move a Smoky Quartz generator crystal six inches above the body as you direct the force of light from the crystal stationary at the crown through the Smoky Quartz. As the Smoky Generator passes above each chakra point, direct a beam of healing energy through the crystal, charging each center as it travels downward. When the Smoky arrives at the base chakra, hold it there for at least three minutes and focus on balancing the higher, more subtle frequencies into the physical body.

As with all dark stones and crystals, Smoky quartz should only be used respectfully and consciously. A great amount of power can be initiated by using this stone and it is very important to know how to direct and channel those energies so that they can serve the highest good. Start by using just one Smoky quartz in crystal healings and as you become more familiar with its force you may add more stones. Always stay in tune with the person you are working with as these stones may need to be removed at a moment's notice if their energies are not being assimilated properly.

BLACK OBSIDIAN

Black Obsidian is one of the most important teachers of all the New Age Stones. It is associated with the first chakra. This energy center pertains to the earth, the physical, to survival, and to the personal ego fulfillment. Black Obsidian acts as a magnet that draws the spirit forces into the body to be governed by the conscious will for use in physical action. When these higher forces are grounded into the world of form it is possible to change the very quality of life on earth by infusing the material plane with more light force. When Black Obsidian is placed on the lower chakra points it draws the finer energies of the higher chakras into the primal centers to be used for ego refinement and purification.

Black Obsidian should only be used when one is educated about its powers and prepared to process the changes that this stone often relentlessly puts one through. Ruled by the planet Pluto, Black Obsidian's purpose is to take the mind through the darkened areas of the subconscious to establish identity in the super-conscious. Being a Plutonian teacher, Black Obsidian does not cater to the ego. Instead, it bluntly and often tactlessly shows the ego-self where it is at and what it needs to change in order to advance to the next step of evolutionary growth. It acts as a mirror that reflects the flaws in one's nature and magnifies the fears, insecurities and egocentric attitudes that suppress the soul's superior qualities. Black Obsidian could be named "the warrior of truth", that which slays the illusion to give birth to the vision of the Aquarian Age. In this new age each person will live in accordance to the dictates of their own higher consciousness and that unified consciousness will form the foundation and be the common denominator that links each person to the same truth.

Black Obsidian is a master teacher and has come to teach us the true meaning of the color black. Black, being the dense, the dark and the unknown, is the polar opposite to the color white, which is the seen, the lightened and the known. Each of these expressions are the exact opposite of the other, and being the soul-mates that they are, they allow the other to exist. Each of these colors has contained within it all other colors; both black and white can potentially contain the same degree of light.

The New Age Stones

With black on one end of the color spectrum and white on the other, the entire panorama of color can come into existence and express the multi-faceted nature of each of these colors. Cradled in the arms of black and white, of day and night, of dark and light, life on earth was conceived, given birth to, and reared and is now ready to come to know that the seemingly opposite poles are in reality the same. The concepts of good and evil are but a trick played on the senses when these colors are seen as separate.

The color black has been more misused and misunderstood than any other color in the entire spectrum. As the human soul has evolved and felt the power of the universe flowing through his veins, he has had a tendency to claim that power for his own. In seeking only personal selfish gratification, he has learned to channel this cosmic force onto the planet in ways that only serve his little ego instead of serving the force itself. When this happens, the light contained within black is turned in upon itself and the lowest aspects of man's nature take over. Black magic is just this type of gross misuse of power that will manifest in evil deeds, satanic influences and demonic energies. But this very process of power abuse is one of the greatest lessons that the universe has to teach its occupants.

The black hole theory can be seen existing within different aspects of creation, from human to stellar. This natural phenomenon is one that is created when light is selfishly consumed and reverted back in upon itself, bringing destruction and devastation on all other surrounding objects as they are drawn into the black hole by an increasingly strong gravitational pull. As the light is sucked up, the void grows deeper and larger until at last the soul or the stars are reborn as they come to know that light is to be shared and equally owned by all. Once this is learned, all of the light that was consumed by the black hole explodes out onto the other side of reality and the white hole exists as a brilliant manifestation of a lesson well learned. Each of us, at one time or another, must go through the black hole process of self-destructiveness and learn how to properly use light and energy. As the mass inhabitants of the entity of earth learn this lesson, the earth as a whole will be reborn and the Aquarian Age will flourish.

Black Obsidian teaches us that the black hole within each of us is the non-identification with the source of light and that it is the darkness of fear and selfishness that leads us to our own self destruction. Black Obsidian will bring light into those fears and prove that they are but an illusion and a misunderstanding of the truth. Black Obsidian's greatest characteristic is its ability to contain and reflect large degrees of light. Unlike some other black stones that tend to absorb light, Black Obsidian attracts and reflects light while conserving and retaining its own dynamic light force. Black Obsidian demonstrates through example how to use the light force properly and respectfully. In doing so it assists in transforming human consciousness to be able to use the cosmic energy to open doors to future possibilities yet unimagined.

Black is one of the highest colors worn by advanced initiates of the secret mystery schools. It symbolizes, as Black Obsidian does, mastery over the physical plane. In the practice and graduating degrees of martial arts the "black belt" is the ultimate achievement attained and represents the ability to properly ground and spontaneously use the chi energy (cosmic force) for self defense.

The New Age Stones

In order to receive the master's degree in life and become as one of the living masters (Christ, Buddha, or Mohammed) it is mandatory that one learn how to overcome the temptation of egocentric power abuse and to be unaffected by the so-called negative influences that living in a dualistic world will constantly present. Black Obsidian demonstrates the ability to be completely identified and one with the light while existing and functioning on the material plane. It exemplifies the ability to maintain a centered meditative state of mind while in the midst of the hustle and bustle of 20th century life. The Black Obsidian consciousness interprets all experiences and occurrences from a neutral clear perspective. The mastery is in the ability to constantly identify with the truth that is inherent, but often hidden in the illusion, in every facet of life. This divine sight enables one to be even more human, more compassionate and more understanding because one knows that no matter what the seeming circumstance or karmic happening, that all is in divine right order and the universe and everything in it eternally exists in a brilliant state of perfection.

In much of the western Christian-Judaic dogma we are led to believe that heaven is a place that we will go if we earn the right and prove ourselves to be "good" while on earth. Black Obsidian has come to boldly announce that heaven is a state of mind capable of being attained while on earth and while in a physical body. Indeed, the true magic and challenge in living is to create heaven while on earth and to transform the very quality of the physical world so that the seeds of heaven will find fertile soil upon this planet and be nurtured and cared for and harvested by the children of earth. As this transformation takes place the very nature of matter will be altered as the atoms which form the substance for physical manifestation will vibrate at a higher frequency, allowing more light to fill the spaces between the atomic protons, neutrons and electrons.

Black Obsidian balls are extremely powerful meditation pieces. Often they will have concentric rings around them and occasionally display beautiful bullseye rings on the northern and southern poles. Caution must be taken before embarking upon a Black Obsidian ball meditation, for the power of these objects cannot be overstated. In a personal meditation experience with a very large Black Obsidian ball, I stared into it for no longer than 90 seconds and had to process the effects for three weeks. Uneducated misuse of Black Obsidian balls can draw one into their own dark nature and should only be used by those prepared to consciously channel its energies. If abused, it could draw one's awareness too deep within itself and drastically alter the auric pattern, breaking down the protective characteristics of the electro-magnetic field. This could create innumerable physical, mental and emotional repercussions. The purpose of these power pieces is to bring to light that which is hidden from the conscious mind, to take the awareness through the darkened areas of the self, to penetrate the unknown and eventually bring the mind to see with the intuitive all-knowing sight. With this third eye vision, one sees that all things are ONE and everything manifests its own unique perfect expression of God's creation. but in the process, be prepared to face fears, programmed patterns, avoided issues and insecurities you didn't know you even had. Be ready to clean out the dirty cobwebs in the darkest corners of your mind. When this purging is complete, the veils of illusion will be lifted, the third eye opened and the ultimate truth known.

Black Obsidian balls should be treated with the greatest respect and kept covered with a silk or velvet cloth when not in use. It is possible to uncover it during crystal healings if the person you are working with sincerely wants to break through a mental barrier but is unable to do so. Always before using, inform your client of its powers and potential effects and ask permission to use it on them. If consent is given, hold the ball six inches above the third eye area for no more than three minutes. This will assist penetration through stubborn subconscious mental blocks.

After using Black Obsidian balls in meditation or in crystal healings, it is advised to .practice a simple clear Quartz meditation once a day for three days afterward to balance and polarize the effects. Clear Quartz serves as a perfect polarity to Black Obsidian (reflecting clear white light) and should be used in conjunction with Black Obsidian when practicing Obsidian ball meditations or using Black Obsidian stones in crystal healings. When gazing into a Black Obsidian ball it is advised to hold a large (at least six inches) Generator Quartz while practicing the meditation. When using Black Obsidian stones in crystal healing layouts it is best to have a small Quartz crystal placed in close proximity for each piece of Black Obsidian used. Clear Quartz will polarize Black Obsidian's intensity and serve to dissolve and neutralize any psychic or emotional debris that is surfaced. When performing crystal healings, Black Obsidian stones may be placed upon the groin points or on the navel to ground higher energies into the body. They also may be placed along the center line of the body to balance the subtle energy flows (meridians).

To summarize, Black Obsidian can teach its students how to bring more light into a darkened world. It will show the mind of the devoted student that all manifestations, no matter how dense in matter, come from the same source and that both black and white are equally powerful forms of light. Black Obsidian is an agent in the interbreeding of a higher form of awareness on this planet. It works by drawing the soul qualities into the body and cleansing anything that is of a lesser vibration. Working with Black Obsidian draws one into their own earth center and into the body to effectively utilize the light force. It is ideal to use on people who are scattered or overly emotional because it stabilizes erratic energies. It is also good to use on people that are very spaced-out or who tend to daydream or fantasize too much. It will help build the foundation upon which daydreams can become living realities. Black Obsidian represents the true earth forces, containing within it the greens, blues and golds indigenous to earth. If used wisely, Black Obsidian will teach you the truth about yourself and the universe of which you are a vital part.

GEM SILICA (CHRYSOCALLA)

"I am Venus, I am beauty and love, I am harmony (we must love to see beauty). I am gentle yet powerful.

You have known me since time began. I am your God instinct, I am compassion and tranquility, I am balance, I am mercy.

Through me creation is idealized and evolves itself to continually higher forms.

I am the Mother, the overseer of the creation. I nourish the seed. I calm the emotions and bring peace to the soul. Through me clarity of purpose triggers projection and crystalization (manifestation). I teach patience and understanding through love and relaxation. I am the receptivity of your divine instinctual consciousness. I am where the cosmic ocean and the cosmic sky meet on the horizon."

(The sky shows the limitless heights of ascension and the ocean points towards the depth of the soul.)

Written by GaryFleck

In the evolution of color, Gem Silica has emerged as one of the highest and clearest color rays in the blue spectrum. In the last few centuries turquoise was the prominent stone that manifested this color frequency. Turquoise was used extensively by the American Indians of the midwest and is still very popular today for use in jewelry and ornamentation. Another stone which displays almost identical color is chrysocolla. Both turquoise and chrysocolla are semi-precious stones, being opaque and rather dull in luster.

On rare occasion, when mining for chrysocolla, veins of gem quality silicates are discovered. Chrysocolla mines are rare (found in New Mexico and

101

South America), but rarer still is the Gem Silica or gem quality Chrysocolla. (If sincerely sought after, however, it will attract itself to the seeker.) Gem Silica is the highest evolved form of the turquoise color, manifesting the deep blue color of the infinite summertime sky and the ocean waters surrounding the Hawaiian Islands. It is clear, transparent, translucent and brilliant to behold, being of precious nature and ranking in quality with Aquamarine, Topaz and Kunzite. Gem Silica is usually hard to locate and fairly expensive.

Gem Silica has claimed its rightful heritage as one of the most beautiful New Age Stones. It has been thousands of years in the making and now emerges in full glory to give its message of peace to the planet. As the human race becomes more receptive to receive the tranquil yet powerful energies that Gem Silica has to offer, it is believed that more Chrysocolla-Gem Silica mines will be discovered to offer this healing blue ray in greater abundance.

Gem Silica is a feminine stone, being the water, the winter, the moon, the passive yet power, the emotions and the yin energies. Pictures or statues of the Divine Mother will usually show her wearing this color. It represents the peaceful compassion that the Mother emanates from her being. Gem Silica vibrates this essence and therefore can be used to develop the virtues of patience, kindness, tolerance, compassion and humility. It also inspires the soul to surrender and yield to the latent divine forces of one's own nature.

Being the feminine energy that it is, Gem Silica is the ideal stone to use in cases of feminine disorders. It is extremely beneficial for women who suffer from menstrual discomfort (backache, cramping, depression) and can assist in balancing the hormones which regulate the menstrual cycle. Gem Silica is one of the best stones to use after miscarriages, abortions, or hysterectomies. It is also ideal to hold, wear or meditate upon during the labor and birth process. To ease menstrual strain or to de-traumatize the tissues after miscarriage, abortion or hysterectomy, place three Gem Silica stones over the uterus-ovary area and one on the third eye center. This will also help neutralize the feelings of sadness or guilt upon having experienced such ordeals.

Gem Silica is an emotional balancer and can be placed over the heart chakra, worn, held, envisioned, or meditated upon to bring erratic or uncontrolled emotional behavior under control of the will. It eases the pain of sorrow and the strain of anger by bringing both to peace, to be replaced by understanding and forgiveness. Being the comforter that it is, Gem Silica is the perfect stone to give or to use with men who are unwilling or unable to allow themselves the privilege of feeling. It will gently nurture the ability to be more vulnerable and sensitive by healing the unresolved emotional wounds responsible for the suppression and closing off of the feeling nature. Gem silica will also assist women to be more motherly, nurturing, understanding, empathetic and compassionate.

Gem Silica brings peace to the mind and heart. It is not just the inner meditative experience of peace but also the active expression of peace where one lives in harmony with him/herself and with the world around them. Peace can only happen when the soul is at peace with itself. As more people experience this, the planet will manifest that reality and outer peace will be reflected in all personal, inter-personal, social and planetary aspects of life. Gem Silica is the "peace stone", for it initiates the inner experience of serenity as it projects that energy into the world to be lived through powerful action in thoughts, feelings, words and deeds.

Gem Silica can be used as a cooling stone to lower fevers, heal burns, neutralize anger and calm frazzled nerves. In any of these cases you may place stones on the body (third eye, heart, and navel), wear them, or hold and meditate upon them, breathing in the Gem Silica blue as you exhale out the unwanted energies.

Gem Silica is a wonderful stone to use in crystal healing layouts. It can activate any of the chakras as it harmonizes and balances the subtle etheric bodies with the physical. Blue is the color for the throat chakra and Gem Silica can be placed upon the throat or neck in cases of thryoid imbalance, voice problems, sore throats or neck and shoulder tension. When placed upon the third eye, Gem Silica acts as a bridge that connects the everyday state of consciousness to the more expanded states of awareness that are usually only attained after years of disciplined mental control and meditation. Just as the daytime sky bridges the earth with the heavens, the deep blue color that Gem silica reflects integrates cosmic consciousness with the common waking state of mind. These qualities have made Gem Silica a favorite as a meditation stone.

To experience the essence of Gem Silica, lie down and place a Gem Silica stone between the eyebrows as you breathe long and deep, allowing the mind to let go of any and all thoughts that may enter the consciousness. As the body relaxes and the mind is calmed, the energies of Gem Silica will lift the awareness to a higher level. In order to fully experience this subtle state of mind, it is important to stay awake and train the mind to be more relaxed than if in sleep while still maintaining the thread of consciousness. Once this bridge is built, it is then possible to have conscious out-of-the-body experiences and come to know the subtle realms as a reality. When practicing this type of meditation it is important to protect yourself by surrounding yourself with white light and asking for divine guidance before embarking upon such a journey. This type of meditation helps develop the eighth chakra, which is an energy center approximately six inches above the top of the head (known as the soul star). When this chakra is activated it will establish the connection between the individual and cosmic forces.

Gem Silica also lends its abilities as a "seeing stone"through which can be seen past and future events. By holding a high quality, exceptionally clear Gem Silica stone between the thumb and the forefinger and gazing into it, images, symbols, scenes and visions will come to life and display themselves in the mirror of the stone. To experience this clairvoyant sight one must lose him/herself into the color and energy of the stone while simultaneously recording into memory what was witnessed. Many prophetic visions can be constructively used to aid in planetary peace if the higher powers of this stone are used properly. As with any of the New Age Power Stones, it is very important that the forces of these transformative tools be used only with the best intentions and humanitarian goals in mind. If misused for personal selfish gain, the karmic repercussions can bring devastation into the life of the abuser. When used properly, Gem Silica can bring peace, harmony, and expansion into one's life and onto the planet.

FLUORITE
(Clusters, Octahedrons, Pyramids)

Fluorite is a multi-dimensional stone. It is the stone that manifests the highest aspect of the mind—the mind that is attuned to spirit. From that exalted state of consciousness comes the intellectual understanding of truth, of cosmic concepts of reality and of the laws that govern the universe.

Fluorite is for the advancement of mind, for developing the ability to comprehend and integrate the non-physical realities of the fourth, fifth and sixth dimensions. When the mind is attuned to the essence of Fluorite, it is possible to experience and know the inner sanctums of the self, where all knowledge and wisdom is contained. Fluorite balances the positive and negative aspects of the mind. When these polarities equalize it is possible to experience the silence and peace of neutrality, merging into the eternal moment, where time stands still and the self unites with the infinite. But the experience of Fluorite goes even one step beyond this. It incorporates this reality into the active mentality of daily living, enabling one to stay attuned to that source while functioning on the physical plane. When this occurs, all of the thoughts that emanate from the conscious or subconscious mind are attuned and aligned with the ultimate source of truth. Fluorite consciousness allows one to maintain awareness of the ONE, the ALL, while still claiming individual unique expression and existence. By doing this it is possible to tap into vast resources of creative energy for manifestation in one's life.

Fluorite is a third eye stone, one that enables the mind to maintain a meditative and centered space while

106

in the midst of physical activity. It is the polarity energy to Amethyst, which is the internal experience of surrendering the mind in order to attain wisdom. Fluorite brings that experience into the day to day thought processes, allowing one to see the reality behind the illusion, the eternal in the transitory and the truth beyond the confusion. Fluorite is one of the most powerful of the New Age Stones, for it brings onto the physical plane higher forms of truth and integrates those concepts into the mind, which in turn manifests on the material plane.

Fluorite is a stone that is not indigenous to earth. It has been transported here from the higher dimensions to assist in our evolutionary process. It is to be used with respect, as are all the stones; if used with awareness, its power can assist in developing high degress of mental capacity.

Fluorite can also be used in treating certain types of mental illness and disturbances in brain wave frequencies. It increases the electrical charge of the brain cells which brings more life force (prana) into the brain, which in turn expands the consciousness. It is not so much for cleansing the subconscious (as Azurite is) but for advancing the mind from one mental reality to the next. Fluorite can be used to develop greater ability to concentrate and if used on a regular basis can nurture the intellect and even raise the IQ. Fluorite's nickname is the "genius stone" for it represents the highest state of mental achievement.

Fluorite manifests in four main colors: blue, purple, gold and white. All of these colors represent meditative states of mind. Blue is the color of inner peace, mental calmness and serenity. Purple represents the devotional aspect of a mind that is focused on and committed to spirit. Gold is the color of wisdom and understanding, where the mind merges with infinity and still maintains individual expression. White is the color of purity and oneness, when the mind completely merges with the universal spirit and experiences the totality of creation. All of the colors represent the upper chakras, the higher triangle of energy, and advanced states of consciousness. When these colors are dominant in the aura (which can occur through the use of Fluorite) the state of mind associated with these colors is activated and the potential of human evolution facilitated.

Fluorite has three different states of manifestation: the cluster, the octahedrons, and the pyramid form. None of these structures are more evolved than the rest; however, each form serves a specific purpose. The clusters usually occur in the purple color. They represent the 21st century computer-age technological mind. Fluorite clusters are much like a computer and are very organized, structured, and complex. They look much like you would imagine an advanced space city to look, their cubical matrix displaying harmonious compatibility of all parts. They subliminally suggest advanced states of consciousness that have learned to survive and grow through mutual cooperation. Fluorite clusters symbolize civilizations that have accomplished unity and harmony by fulfilling the needs of each individual and aligning personal goals to comply with the needs of the whole.

Fluorite clusters represent the phase of human existence where the intellectual mind utilizes its technologies in conjunction with universal will for the betterment of all. Let's see how we evolved to this place. As early man learned to use tools that made his lifestyle easier, he no longer needed to focus all of his attention on physical survival, thus further allowing his mental faculties to develop. In the industrial revolution machines replaced physical human labor and enabled the mind of man to develop even more. As the human mind now expands into the space age it has learned to transfer knowledge into living machines (computers) which in turn are programmed to serve human needs. As humankind experiences this extreme technological advancement and stores its intellectual thought processes into computers, we are then able to take the next evolutionary step over the threshold into higher realms of thought. The computer age will hopefully replace mental labor and allow the spirit to develop. Caution must be taken in this phase of mental advancement and in those persons of high mindedness and advanced intellect so that the focus remains on the source of all knowledge and the mutual benefit of its use for all. Fluorite clusters say just that and manifest it as a reminder of the possibility.

Fluorite clusters are not so much for laying on (even though they can be used in that way) but more for their physical presence in working areas, such as on desks, in laboratories or in places of study and research. Their presence reminds the mind to stay focused, organized, clear and in-tune. Small clusters can be carried or worn on the person and visually, mentally or physically tuned into if the mind becomes tired, confused or imbalanced. Meditating upon Fluorite clusters will initiate conscious mental clarity, capable of grasping concepts and realities that otherwise might be inaccessible. They create mental order and assist the mind to remain clear and focused while in the midst of activity. Clusters are beneficial for people who live life at a fast pace, who physically and mentally exert large amounts of energy. They are for scientists, physicists, chemists, engineers, computer designers and programmers, executives, business people, accountants and students. They are for anyone who works under pressure and wants to keep the mind clear and calm. Fluorite clusters are especially good for people who are working with the complexities of the 20th century technology, for it assists the mind to direct that knowledge in a way that will be beneficial for the entire planet and all living things.

As the cluster evolves the single octahedrons grow from it. The octahedron represents the quality of the individual that is bred when nurtured in the advanced society of the cluster. It is an eight-sided structure, each side a perfect equilateral triangle, joining forces at six terminations. Each of the terminations can form the apex for a four-sided double pyramid shape, sharing together a common base. This dual pyramid effect symbolizes the completion achieved when the energies of the higher subtle realms merge and are integrated with the physical plane. Any way that you choose to turn an octahedron it will display the double pyramid effect with the apex of the upper and lower pyramids connecting the higher and lower planes. Octahedrons have come into our presence as symbols, tools, and reminders of our own potential completeness, when we too will exist in a state of oneness and balance our inner and outer worlds.

Fluorite octahedrons come in varying sizes, ranging from 1/8 inch to one foot at the base. They sometimes manifest in shades of pink and green (heart colors) which could be used to bring an understanding to more emotional affairs. Smaller octahedrons are generally inexpensive and can be found in quantity at gem and mineral shows or shops carrying mineral specimens. They can

110

easily be used in jewelry, carried, meditated upon as symbols, or placed in obvious places as reminders of unity. They are also beneficial to use in crystal healings. A simple fluorite balancing is done by lying face up and holding an octahedron in each hand with one placed above each eyebrow. This will balance the hemispheres of the brain and clear the mind of unwanted mental debris (also see Fluorite Layout, Chapter III).

The pyramid form of Fluorite is for meditation and should be used for such. These special structures are intended to serve specific purposes and do not like to sit idly and collect dust. They are for those who are ready to move into the inner realms of being and experience the formlessness within the form. Many fluorite pyramids, when held up to the light, display inner sanctums that resemble chambers that descend deeper within. When these are meditated upon the mind is drawn to seek deeper within itself.

The pyramid form is a statement of perfection and balance. It is one of the highest geometrical shapes found on the physical plane. It represents conscious connection with the infinite source of energy at the apex and complete groundedness and physical stability at the base. Pyramids are symbolic of the ultimate balance that each soul must achieve to complete its evolutionary process. Egyptian and Aztec pyramids were used for the purpose of channeling cosmic forces onto the physical plane, giving initiates the experience of cosmic awareness. They still stand unto this day as a reminder and a message to the world that unity exists, not only within the individual human being but within the universe itself. Fluorite pyramids can serve much the same purpose by training the mind to associate and identify with the reality of the inner realms, the subtle planes and the higher dimensions. These conscious meditative experiences can drastically change the quality of day to day life by enabling one to gain clearer perspective and greater understanding of the universal laws that govern the physical laws.

To practice the Fluorite pyramid meditation, place your pyramid piece so it is level with your third eye area. It is best to have the Fluorite pyramid on a light box with light shining up through it or with natural or artificial light shining through it from the back. This will bring to life the inner chambers of the pyramid. Sit in a cross-legged position with a very straight spine and the arms straight with the palms face up on the knees. Imagine yourself to be a pyramid with the top of your head being the apex and your crossed legs forming the base. Sit straight and still, breathing deeply with the eyes closed for three minutes. Then very slightly open the eyes and gaze into the pyramid for the same length of time. Allow the mind to travel deep within the pyramid and experience the essence of the Fluorite energy and the perfected pyramid form. Then again close the eyes and take that image deep within your own mind. Stay as concentrated as possible as you transfer your vision back and forth from the Fluorite pyramid to the inner mind. Continue in this fashion for at least three rounds and end the meditation by breathing deeply and powerfully for at least three minutes as you integrate that image and energy into your physical body. This meditation helps you to open your crown chakra (gateway to the higher realms) and channel that cosmic energy into your physical body to utilize in your day to day life.

It is possible, while practicing this meditation, to experience past or future lives and realities. As the mind becomes calm, focused and clear, and the polarities balance, the limitations of the third dimension of time and space are transcended. When this occurs the eternal moment is witnessed which contains all times, all spaces and all experiences. It is the state of mind that unifies the entire universe; where the oneness of all creation can be experienced. In this state of mind it is possible to travel to any place and anytime by simply willing it. When traveling at the speed of thought it is not necessary to go through space or time, you simply think it and you are there. In these special moments it is possible to see how past life effects (karmas) create the reality of the present and how the present projections create future probabilities. This state of consciousness is the potential of the Fluorite experience and takes concentrated and devoted meditative practice to achieve. It is possible when you learn to create a state of mind that is silent and still, yet simultaneously moving so fast that it is beyond motion. Having transcended the laws of the third dimension, it is then possible to project and enforce the laws of the fourth dimension onto the physical plane third dimensional world.

Fluorite, in all of its forms, is here to teach us to be inter-dimensional. It can show us how to be at one and in a state of peace while still being individually unique; and how to incorporate infinity into each moment. It is the symbol of the growth process that we are all involved in; of aligning with the cosmic force and source of our being and accepting the responsibility to live in the Divine Will and manifest Light through physical action.

KUNZITE

In many ways the heart chakra is the most important of all the energy centers. It is located in the center of the body and governs the balance of the upper three and lower three chakras. If the heart chakra is clear and open, all of the other chakras come into alignment with it. The heart extends its circulation to the entire body and all systems and tissues are nurtured with vital force. Just as the heart pumps oxygenated blood to feed all of the body's cells, the heart chakra radiates its dynamic influence to all the chakra centers. Kunzite manifests the matured state of heart; open, clear, secure, strong, vibrant, radiant, balanced and loving. As Kunzite grows in popularity, it indicates that more people are evolving to the point where they can and will reach the full potential of their own heart.

Fluorite manifests the state of inner mental balance and Kunzite expresses emotional equilibrium. Fluorite escorts the consciousness into the inner sanctums of the mind while Kunzite enables the inner dimensions of the heart to be experienced. Kunzite will connect one to their own infinite source of love. In natural form Kunzite has parallel striations running the length of the crystal. Whenever you see striations like this (see Tourmaline) it indicates that energy will move through the stone at an extremely rapid rate. This accelerated motion of energy will automatically raise the vibration of any surrounding elements. In doing so, many lower negative energies are dissolved and dissipated.

Kunzite is one of the main heart chakra trinity stones. Its purpose is to prepare the internalized self-love (which Rose Quartz has initiated) to be offered in external expression. This stage of development involves a total surrender and letting go of the fears and sorrows that bind the heart to the past, or to anxious anticipation of the future. Kunzite is an ever-active state of the present, existing in the perfection of the moment. When Kunzite is placed or worn over the heart chakra points, its energy penetrates through emotional blockages and allows one to experience the purity of their own inner heart. Since the soul abides in the body at the heart chakra, the Kunzite experience gives one direct contact with their own essence.

When Kunzite is observed closely, both pale pink and light purple color rays can be found. This represents the ability that Kunzite has to create a balance between the mind (purple) and the heart (pink). Kunzite will channel its energy from the heart into the head to transform the thought patterns that are associated with emotional blockage. Only when both the thoughts and the feelings attached to those thoughts are neutralized, can a complete healing occur.

Kunzite will usually reflect a clear ray of light pale pink. In gem quality, Kunzite manifests the purest transparency of any stone in the pink spectrum. This crystal clarity is the main reason Kunzite has earned its place as one of the New Age Stones. It symbolizes a pure expression of joy in thoughts and feelings. It is the state of activated self love that has been made ready to freely give, unconditionally, without demands or expectations. When used in conjunction with pink Tourmaline, Kunzite's cheerful light heartedness is directed out into the world.

Kunzite also offers itself as a powerful personal meditation stone. It can be used to balance negative emotional states and/or troubled mental states. To practice this meditation, sit with the straight spine and hold a piece of Kunzite to the center of the chest. As you inhale, fill the heart with Kunzite's purifying energy. Hold the breath momentarily as you visualize a pink ray rising up to the third eye center. As it reaches the brow, exhale and mentally project a light purple-pink ray back into the heart. Continue in this fashion for 11 minutes and marvel at the results. This meditation will clear the mind, calm the emotions, and leave you in a peaceful state of balance.

When Kunzite is placed on the heart chakra during crystal healings, a Clear Quartz Generator Crystal can be rotated in a clockwise direction two to three inches above it. This will guide the Kunzite force into the inner realms of the heart and seal the aura against negative outside influences. If you remain very focused, the terminated end of the quartz crystal can come to rest directly on top of the Kunzite stone. At this time, channel your own healing thoughts through the crystal. This will charge the Kunzite with even greater force. This is an advanced technique and should only be used when the recipient is ready and able to consciously let go of their fears. Charging Kunzite with a Clear Quartz in this manner raises the energy to such a high frequency that it will cut through any blockages that bind and constrict the heart chakra.

Kunzite is an ideal stone to give to children who are having a hard time adjusting to and functioning in life. Kunzite's soft pink ray will comfort their hearts and cleanse any auric shadows that have accumulated by being in dirty or negative vibrations. Kunzite is also a good stone to be worn by star children or walk-ins to help them adjust to earth plane environments and energy.

Kunzite is a special gift to our earth. Its presence emits a deep sense of peace and balance. It is the expression of the evolved open heart that understands all things, that is above and beyond attachment, that knows utter compassion and that is eternally free from fear.

RHODOCHROSITE

In a time when it is of vital importance to integrate spiritual and material energies, Rhodochrosite has made its specialized qualities known. In doing so, it has become one of the main contributors and harbingers to the New Age. This stone harmoniously blends the colors of pink and orange, creating a beautiful peach color. When this combination of color frequencies merge, birth is given to a new color ray, one that serves a very specific purpose.

Orange-yellow is the color associated with the navel chakra, or the power of the earth and the physical body. Pink is the vibration of the heart chakra and represents the capacity to feel selfless love and compassion. The navel forms the apex for the lower three chakras, known as the lower triangle, or the lower triad of energy. The heart chakra forms the base for the upper chakras, the love of the heart being the foundation upon which spirituality and higher consciousness is built. The upper four chakras form the upper triangle, or the higher energy centers. Between the upper energy centers and the lower ones is the solar plexus, located underneath the sternum and encompasses the diaphragm and lower rib region (see chart, page 165). The solar plexus is one of the most sensitive and vulnerable areas of the body. It is where one feels the "butterflies" when nervous and where one becomes tight when feeling anxious. The solar plexus is the center of emotional activity and tends to record and store unresolved emotional conflicts and traumas. When the solar plexus becomes constricted and blocked with suppressed feelings, energy is unable to flow smoothly between the upper and lower energy centers. Rhodochrosite is the God-sent deliverer whose purpose and mission it is to clear the solar plexus and integrate the energies of the physical and spiritual realms.

When a child takes its first breath, one of the most important physiological changes that occurs is the movement of the diaphragm. This powerful muscle, attached to the bottom of the ribs, descends as air is pulled into the lower lungs and contracts as it pushes the air out. Subconsciously, the child associates this diaphragmatic motion with life itself and with the personal exchange of energy that it has with the outside world. Small infants, when lying face up, demonstrate the ability to breathe fully and completely. Regulated by the smooth action of the diaphragm, the breath can be seen filling the lower abdominal and pubic cavities on each inhale and fluidly releasing the energy on the exhale. When the breath is deep and complete, the prana (life energy) taken in with each breath energizes each of the chakras as it circulates throughout the entire system. But when life experiences become painful or traumatic, the breath will automatically become shortened and shallow. This subconscious attempt to avoid drawing into the body disagreeable circumstances results in constriction of the diaphragm, suppression of emotion at the solar plexus, and a loss of vital force in the body. This type of energy blockage then becomes responsible for many physical problems such as stomach ulcers, breath and lung problems (asthma), digestive disorders, constipation and a disintegrated sense of being. In order to heal any of these symptoms it is necessary to first release the emotional stresses which have created the problem and then retrain the body to breathe properly as the heart is retrained to assimilate life experiences without closing off. The vibrant yet soothing color of Rhodochrosite is for the physical as well as the emotional healing that must take place in order to truly change the patterns of disease. Therefore, Rhodochrosite is an ideal stone to use for any of the above listed disorders.

As the energy of Rhodochrosite is infiltrated into the aura, a spiritualizing process begins to occur whereby the higher energies of the upper chakras are stimulated and directed into the lower centers. At the same time the physical systems are activated and become more receptive to assimilate the higher frequencies. As the bridging of the upper and lower chakras takes place, one becomes empowered on the physical plane to consciously utilize the creative faculties of the higher energy centers.

Rhodochrosite works very well in conjunction with Malachite. The drawing force of Malachite will surface suppressed emotional energies so that the comforting and harmonizing characteristics of Rhodochrosite can be put to use. Both of these stones are ideal to use together in crystal healing layouts. Place Malachite or Rhodochrosite stones anywhere along the midline of the body between the navel and the heart center to clear and balance the chakras. Rhodochrosite is especially beneficial to use directly over the solar plexus point (directly beneath the sternum, between the ribs) to serve as a bridge between the lower and upper triads.

Rhodochrosite is often found with white lines or white whisps running through it. This symbolizes the

119

power that this mineral has to channel the white light energy from the crown chakra into the physical body. Rhodochrosite can be found in many shades of peach, ranging from pale pink to dark orange. Stones are usually cut and polished by a lapidary artist but can also be found in natural slabs. Rhodochrosite crystals and clusters are rare but can occasionally be found at large gem and mineral shows. These collector's items are well worth the high price as they crystallize in brilliant form the highest essence of Rhodochrosite. Also rare is the gem quality Rhodochrosite which is usually a much darker shade of orange and transparently beautiful. Gem quality crystals or stones can be used in remedy form to purify the bloodstream in cases of toxification. An elixir made from deep red-orange Rhodochrosite crystals can be of considerable value in cancer treatment and liver purification.

Rhodochrosite is most appealing when it is worn as jewelry. When this stone is worn in gem quality, its transparent essence vibrates the consciousness and raises it into the realm of spiritual awareness. When worn in the semi-precious state, it channels the spiritual awareness into the physical body to be manifested. Gem quality or semi-precious stones can also be used for the same purposes in crystal healing layouts. In either form, for either purpose, spirit becomes better integrated with matter.

Another positive healing attribute of Rhodochrosite is its ability to help restore poor eyesight. Often the reasons for impaired vision arise from a person "not wanting to see" or acknowledge certain elements in life or in their personal experiences. These attitudes of avoidance and denial can eventually affect the eyesight. In such cases, small Rhodochrosite stones can be placed around the eyes to help a person accept, positively interpret, assimilate, and integrate what they see and how they feel about what is seen.

Gem quality Rhodochrosite can be used in meditation to focus on the soul's purpose and to gain clarification as to one's personal mission in life. Stones or crystals can be held in the left hand or placed up to the third eye center during meditation to receive their personal message. Rhodochrosite stones can be placed or held on points over the eyebrows, the temples and/or the center suture in the head to stimulate the brain, allowing more spirit energy to inhabit the physical body and infiltrate the thought processes.

SUGILITE
(Also Known as *Luvulite* and Royal Lazel)

Even though the common name for this special stone is Sugilite, for sentimental purposes we will refer to it as "Luvulite".

Luvulite has only surfaced on this planet in the last decade; up until now the human race has not been ready for the deep purple ray that Luvulite reflects. Unlike the transparent crystalline purple that Amethyst displays, Luvulite is usually dense, non-translucent and opaque. The purple color is deep, dark and purposeful.

Luvulite grounds the etheric purple ray deep into the earth, making it more accessible for physical healing. Purple and indigo are colors for the third eye center. The purple ray that Luvulite manifests represents the link that the mind has with the physical body. The mind, and the thoughts emanating from the mind, to a large degree determine the health of the physical body. Luvulite is a New Age Stone whose purpose is to establish conscious control over the mental faculties and in doing so gain the healing power necessary to balance the physical body. Luvulite, when placed upon the third eye center, will show to the sincere student why they have created their physical imbalances and what lessons are involved in the experience. Coming to this realization, it is then possible to clear and release the mental and emotional correlations to the physical dis-ease which will allow the body to then manifest a state of health.

One of the most horrifying and devastating dis-eases on the planet today is cancer. Being a twentieth century illness, cancer is definitely stress related and can manifest in many forms and attack any part of the physical body. The prevalent presence of this dis-ease in our society is a very good indicator that people are unable to release the pressures in their lives. Old angers, resentments, fears, frustrations, guilts, sorrows or insecurities, if not dealt with properly, can build up and create such turmoil in the system that the body can no longer handle the strain and breaks down under the internal pressure. Luvulite is the pressure release valve that can bring peace and understanding to a mind and body that have lost their own source of strength. Luvulite attunes one to their mental body to see what is creating the physical problem. In doing this, the mind can then take the reins and gain control over the physical and channel high amounts of healing energy into the body. This healing force, if used properly, has the power to heal any dis-ease and restore complete mental and physical health.

Luvulite is one of the best stones to be used by very sensitive open people. High minded and well intended

122

souls are often overwhelmed by the intensity of the negative vibrations and influences on this planet. These people are also very susceptible to terminal illnesses because they are unable to understand why the world is the way that it is. In their desperation and hopelessness they will often subconsciously choose death over endurance. Wearing, meditating with, or carrying Luvulite will help bring about a spiritual-mental understanding to the gross physical level and in so doing enable one to spread more light and love into the world. Luvulite is the stone of high awareness that tones the purple ray down to be utilized in the grass roots of the physical plane.

Many super-sensitive evolved beings are being born into the world at this time. These pure children are the lightworkers of the New Age and have a very definite purpose and mission. Luvulite will help these precious souls integrate into the world and will offer them protection against any harmful energies that they might be exposed to. It would be of benefit to place a Luvulite stone under the pillow while a child is sleeping or to carry one when the child goes out into the world. The Luvulite essence will teach the child how to adjust to any circumstances while staying perfectly balanced with their own lighted center. Luvulite is a stone to use to keep the innocence, wisdom and magic of the child's world as they grow into adulthood. It is also an ideal stone to use to reawaken those vital qualities within adults who have forgotten how to relate on those levels.

When using Luvulite in crystal healings, stones can be placed upon the forehead to connect the mind to the wisdom of the third eye. Then the mind can become the key to understanding why the manifestation of dis-ease has occurred and what mental and emotional correlations need to be corrected and balanced in order to bring about a complete and total healing. When working with Luvulite the mind becomes attuned to the spirit which in turn channels its healing force back through the mind and into the body. The lighter paler Luvulite stones are especially good to place over the lymph glands to cleanse and purify the system. They can be placed on the groin, under the arms, along the clavicals or over the spleen and liver to cleanse toxic blood conditions. It can also be used in conjunction with Amethyst over the third eye center to usher the mind into meditative states, capable of tapping incredible wisdom. This quality makes Luvulite a perfect stone to hold or wear while practicing meditation or prayer.

Because of the limited quantity of Luvulite on the planet at this time and its growing popularity, it may be a challenge to locate this valuable stone, and when you do the price will probably be high. But it is well worth the perseverance and the price. Luvulite can be found in beautifully cut cabachons, high quality faceted stones, hand carved symbols or natural rough pieces. When choosing the stone for your use, place Luvulite to your third eye and let it communicate to your intuition if it is the proper stone for your use at this time. Trust the response you receive and enjoy working with this powerful stone.

Luvulite brings to the earth the essence of the purple ray and with it all of the gifts of wisdom and devotion. Luvulite makes possible the transference of energy from the highest most subtle levels of our being into our physical reality, and helps us be multi-faceted in the creative ways that we use that essence in our lives. As we learn to tap our own infinite resources, Luvulite will teach us how to use that power in the wisest of ways. Luvulite carries the message of the heavens to the earth and assists us to integrate those spiritual energies into our daily life. Working with, wearing or meditating with Luvulite gives one the power to channel high frequency purple ray energy into every aspect of living. Consequently, it loves to be set in the purest of gold and surrounded with diamonds to display the regality that it represents.

Luvulite has no doubts about who it is and what it is here for. It has a stable connection with its own source of light and can therefore teach the sincere student how to establish the connection with his/her own source of inner light. Luvulite will display to the open mind how easy it is to be humble when you are identified with the infinite source of energy. Then you realize you are only a very small part of the cosmic whole, yet vital and important, expressing your own unique presence in creation. Luvulite helps you feel good about yourself by dispelling any self doubt or insecurities that keep you from identifying with your own Godliness. Luvulite says "your presence is very important here and you are loved by the forces of life itself. Know, and be who you are and walk on the earth in grace and strength." Luvulite is the chalis into which the holy grail is poured, it is the wisdom that is contained within every atom and within each soul. The presence of Luvulite on the planet at this time indicates that it is now prime time to tap the resources of the soul and come into alignment with the eternal self.

As mankind evolves into a more enlightened state, greater quantities of gem quality Luvulite will be discovered which will be clear, transparent and reflecting the depth of spirit. Then the purple ray will manifest its complete glorious expression on this planet as it transports the wisdom of the universe into the very soil of the earth.

TOURMALINE

Tourmaline is one of the most intense and beautiful stones available on the earth today. Its popularity has grown immensely in the last ten years as many people, either consciously or subconsciously, are drawn to its innate ability to raise the vibration of that which is around it. When Tourmaline is observed closely, long striated lines can be seen protruding in parallel perfection. This geometric design is one of the reasons Tourmaline possesses so much power. The lines channel electrical beams of light that will immediately transform denser vibrations into positive currents of energy. Tourmaline can be used whenever and wherever you want to increase the light force. It can be placed in altars, over chakra points, in children's rooms, in or around plants, in temples or churches or worn as jewelry. Tourmaline stones can be placed between the chakras during crystal healings to bridge the energy from one chakra to the next It is especially good to use in conjunction with Rhodochrosite and Malachite at the solar plexus to integrate the upper energy centers with the lower ones.

The highly charged electrical current that moves rapidly along Tourmaline striations will increase one's own charisma and radiance if worn or used regularly. Exquisite Tourmaline jewelry can be designed and made for purposes of directing the cosmic force into one's being.

Tourmaline energy will weave an intricate fabric of light into the aura. With threads of joy, strength, peace and compassion interwoven into one's nature, it is easy to appreciate the essence that Tourmaline offers. One of the purposes of Tourmaline is to transmit higher virtues and important laws of the universe onto the earth. That is why Tourmaline is so abundant in the 1980's. Tourmaline can teach the peoples of earth to expand and transform limited concepts of thinking into a much finer reality; one that is now far beyond our grasp. Tourmaline has a very specific message and it is, "Align yourself with the forces of light and channel that radiance onto your world and into your life." Tourmaline exemplifies and manifests this ability as it boldly states that not only is it possible, but it is the very destiny of the human race.

Tourmaline surrounds one with a strong protective shield. This will enable one to grow from within while developing the discipline necessary to extend that light to the external world. Tourmaline expresses inner and outer balance and gladly shares its genuine qualities with you.

Tourmaline is one of the most complete stones on the planet at this time It has the ability to reflect all rays of the color spectrum, from clear white to the deepest black. Tourmaline adjusts its vibration to manifest a perfect expression of each color. In so doing, Tourmaline demonstrates the ability to be multi-faceted in the expression of light.

Tourmaline builds the bridge upon which the earth can merge with the heavens and the subtle energy bodies can align with the physical. It creates a balance of forces by lowering the frequency of spirit and raising the frequency of denser matter. This creates a harmonious interbreeding of cosmic and material energies.

Tourmaline is one of the stones that is not indigenous to earth. It has been materialized on our planet by higher life forms to assist the human transition into the Aquarian Age. Tourmaline will build the rainbow bridge upon which the soul can traverse and express its multi-dimensional forms. It creates an equilibrium of forces by raising the material frequency and lowering the spiritual vibration, linking the different worlds together as one.

Tourmaline Wands

Wands are one of the most astonishing forms of this inter-dimensional mineral. Being long, slender, clear and naturally terminated, Tourmaline wands channel high powered electrical energy. If used consciously, these wands are capable of performing miracles. By properly directing the positive force of these tools of light, physical laws can be transcended and phenomenal healing can occur. In personal experience, I have witnessed a multicolored blue Tourmaline wand rejuvenate what was medically defined as total nerve damage. It took several intense crystal healing sessions to heal a woman who had suffered complete loss of movement in her left arm due to a car accident. After charging the nerve and meridian pathways with the wand, she could once again feel impulses and eventually move her arm.

With adequate training, Tourmaline wands can be used along the skull suture lines and specific points on the head to stimulate certain types of brain activity. This advanced technique could be likened to futuristic laser beam brain surgery in which old, unuseful mental processes are erased and replaced with better thought patterns. This type of therapy would facilitate the transformation of destructive habits in criminals and maladjusted juveniles.

Naturally terminated Tourmaline wands are eagerly sought after by many and are expensive, but are well worth the investment. Wands can be found in solid or graduating colors. Some Tourmaline wands are up to eight inches long and reflect a rainbow of color. The clearer the wands are, the higher the electrical voltage they can carry. If one is sensitive and receptive, it is possible to feel the dynamic force that is channeled through these magic wands.

It is believed that in alchemical laboratories deep in the Andes in South America, special Tourmaline wands are being created. The enlightened beings who perform such magic dematerialize these precious wands, transport and rematerialize them into mines in South America. These exclusive items, once mined, then attract themselves to the right people at the right time. The power that these wands possess cannot be overstated. Some of them are as large as 12 inches, perfectly terminated and manifesting the full color spectrum, from black at the base to a terminated peak of white. These tools of light are drawn to the ones who intuitively know how to use them. They should be protected and kept safe at all times. These magic wands, if properly used, will vibrate all of the chakras simultaneously as they align the consciousness with the ominpotent cosmic force.

Green Tourmaline
(Verdelite)

This stone is a healer on all levels, extending its energy from the finest subtle spiritual essence to the grossest material form. Green Tourmaline is capable of purifying and strengthening the nervous system enabling it to carry greater amounts of spirit force. As the physical body alters its frequency to adjust to green Tourmaline energy, the hormonal balance shifts to accomodate greater electrical force. As more energy is carried within the physical system, higher degrees of consciousness can be maintained. Green Tourmaline wands can be used to trace meridian lines and nerve pathways to charge the electrical systems of the body. Green Tourmaline is an excellent stone to use or wear to relieve chronic fatigue and exhaustion. Its constant rejuvenating qualities make it the most favorable of all the green life-giving stones. Green Tourmaline will attract towards the user or wearer abundance and prosperity.

Ranging in shade from pale light green to the darkest tones of emerald, green Tourmaline offers a wide variety of uses. Some artists wear green Tourmaline to inspire creativity. Some people use it to seal auric holes that make them vulnerable to negative influences. Many use green Tourmaline to strengthen the ability to project, create and manifest their goals. However it is used, green Tourmaline will adjust itself to meet the specific needs of the individual.

Pink Tourmaline
(Rubellite)

Pink Tourmaline is one of the heart chakra trinity stones. It can be used in conjunction with Rose Quartz and Kunzite to initiate complete activation of the heart chakra. Rose Quartz first focuses on the development of self love which Kunzite then activates and makes ready for external expression. With this foundation prepared, pink Tourmaline can then exert its influence to make a glorious offering of that love to the world. Pink Tourmaline is the giver of love in the material realm. Its very presence creates joy and enthusiasm for life. Pink Tourmaline jubilantly announces that it is safe to love and OK to care and express feelings. Pink Tourmaline is self protected by its own infinite source of compassion which knows no fear or holding back. It dynamically transforms the barriers that bind the heart to sorrow and fear.

Using, carrying, meditating upon or wearing Pink Tourmaline will inspire the heart to release past sorrows and trust once again in the power of love. Many dis-eases originate and have deep roots in emotional pain. The vibrant pink of Tourmaline vibrates the heart chakra at a frequency that will dissolve and dissipate those old destructive stored feelings (see Pink Tourmaline Spiral Layout, Chapter III). Once the heart is cleared of these past impressions it can then come to know the true purpose for feeling: to express the exuberance and joy of love.

Pink Tourmaline varies in color from deep red to light clear rose. Each hue provides a slightly different purpose but all are devoted to serving the highest aspects of the heart.

Black Tourmaline
(known as Schorl)

Black Tourmaline deflects negative energies instead of absorbing them. It is a stone that can be used, worn or carried when going into negative environments or when expecting to come into contact with dense or heavy energies. Black Tourmaline helps form a shield that immunizes one against the effects of harmful physical or psychic influences. It can also be used to neutralize one's own negative energies, i.e. anger, resentment, jealousy, insecurity, etc. By carrying or wearing a piece of Black Tourmaline, neurotic tendencies are drastically reduced.

The vibrant black that Tourmaline reflects is radiant with light. It is one of the best stones to use when trying to ground spiritual energies. It is an ideal stone to place on the lower chakra points during crystal healings to channel and utilize energies into the physical body from the higher chakras. Black Tourmaline wands can be placed at the knees or feet, with terminations facing toward the toes, to direct negative energies out of the body. Black wands can also be used to direct energies from the crown to the base chakras. If there is blockage anywhere in the auric or physical body, black Tourmaline wands can be held above the constricted area and rotated in a counter-clockwise direction to clear and release the constricted energies. When practicing this technique, it is advised to also direct at least three Clear Quartz crystals toward the affected area to help dissolve the blockage.

Black Tourmaline can also be found living in Clear Quartz (called Tourmalined Quartz). The combination of clear white and radiant black creates a perfect polarity of energies. Tourmalined Quartz can be used to eliminate almost any degree of subtle or physical negative energy. It is a manifestation of light and dark forces uniting together to serve a common goal.

Black Tourmaline is a devoted servant to the light and works diligently to bring a clearer expression of light into the world and into the lives of those who are drawn to use its powers. Black Tourmaline will teach its students how to remain radiant in the darkest of circumstances and how to maintain a spiritual consciousness while living in the midst of large polluted cities and being surrounded by unconscious people. It will share its secrets of how to plant seeds in the minds of people that will eventually sprout into blossoms of greater awareness.

Bi, Tri, and Multi-Colored Tourmaline

Bi, tri and multi-colored pieces are a pleasure to behold and a joy to work with. Tourmaline offers a clear reflection of all colors in the spectrum and creatively combines and mixes them. Some Tourmaline pieces display as many as four or five different colors. Tourmaline wands often manifest several graduating hues of the same color. This ability to unite several colors together in the same stone symbolizes the possibility of many nations, races and peoples living together in harmony. Each color is a perfect expression of itself as it adjusts to and respects the rights of the other colors to share the same stone. You can find deep maroons living beautifully with greens, and pinks and blues harmoniously sharing the same space.

One of the best color schemes to work with in crystal healing layouts is the pink/green combination. This bi-colored Tourmaline team is the best heart chakra healer around. The green ray heals the emotional wounds the heart has stored while the pink inspires the love to flow within and without. Working together, pink/green Tourmaline serves to simultaneously pull the weeds while it plants new seeds. This type of Tourmaline can be used in crystal healings on or around the heart chakra as well as the solar plexus area. It will rejuvenate and refresh the heart suffering from the knocks and blows of life. This important bi-colored stone helps build a sense of humor for those who take life too seriously. It lightens the load so that the true inner beauty can be seen, felt and expressed.

CHAPTER V

SUMMARY STATEMENTS ON OTHER IMPORTANT HEALING STONES

This chapter contains a summary statement on the effects and energies of other important healing stones. Many of these stones are "power stones of the ages" that have been used for thousands of years for their healing qualities and some are stones of lesser reputation and heritage. All of these stones can be used in crystal healing layouts and some may even serve particular individual needs more than the New Age Stones do. As always, when working with the healing properties of stones, select the ones that best suit the needs of the person you are working with. Some people may be better able to assimilate the energies of these stones than that of the higher frequency New Age Stones. All of the following stones are indigenous to earth and can be used to transform the basic nature of the human being, enabling greater access and assimilation to the finer energies of the self.

These stones, as well as the ones listed in the chart on pages 160–162, are major contributors in the transformation process and can be used in healing work, meditation, remedies or jewelry.

AMBER

Amber is not a crystalline form nor can it be literally classified as a stone. In actuality, Amber is petrified pine tree sap that is millions of years old. Captured within the sap are frequently found small insects, flowers, seeds and other remnants of prehistoric nature. These preserved life forms make amber an archeological find worth studying.

Amber does not emit strong healing energy, but it does have the power to draw dis-ease from the body. It is beneficial to place pieces of Amber over any area of the body that is imbalanced or in pain. Amber can absorb the negative energy and help the body to heal itself. Often, after using Amber for such purposes, it will become very dull and clouded. Always cleanse Amber after using it to ensure its healing potency and to prevent it from distributing negative energy.

In healing, Amber is mostly used for its brilliant golden color reflection. By placing amber over the area of internal organs, these tissues can be revitalized. The gold-orange color is associated with the navel chakra and the grounding of energies into the physical body. Amber can be worn or used by people that tend to have suicidal tendencies, who do not want to be in a physical body, or who get depressed easily. It will help ground the higher energies onto the earth plane to be utilized by the body for healing and balancing. Amber can be made into stunning jewelry that can be worn for beauty, as well as for grounding and stabilizing effects.

AZURITE

There comes a time in the evolution of each soul when it becomes necessary to challenge the very nature of one's own personal reality. By letting go of old programmed belief systems, it is then possible to take a quantum leap to a greater reality and experience the expanded awareness that comes when outdated concepts are replaced with a deeper understanding of life. Azurite is for that leap. It represents the light as it dissolves the darkness of each fear and transforms it into clearer understanding. Its radiant deep indigo blue color has the ability to move subconscious thoughts into the conscious mind. As mental patterns surface they can then be objectively reviewed and tested against a purer touchstone for truth; one that is founded in greater insight and perspective. Azurite motivates higher thinking by surfacing deep subconscious thought patterns to be examined by the conscious awareness. This process renews, refreshes, and remotivates the thinking to serve a higher purpose.

In ancient Egyptian times this valuable stone was used by the high priests and priestesses in order to raise their awareness to a God-conscious state. Today it can serve a similar purpose. Only now its energies are more grounded to assist us in creating heaven on earth by renewing the belief in our own inner source of light. In the evolutionary process Azurite has become more dense but is no less brilliant or powerful.

The purity of Azurite crystals cleanses the mind and soul and brings light and truth to replace outdated belief systems. This deep vibrant blue has the ability to move healing energy through all levels of one's being—from the physical to the most subtle. Azurite acts as a catalyst to initiate the transformation that integrates the earth with the ethers, the physical with the spiritual. This bridging occurs when the subconscious mind is cleansed, enabling the inner light to be infused into thoughts, feelings, words and actions.

Natural gem-quality Azurite wands, on special occasions, can be found at gem and mineral shows and are most precious and powerful tools. The terminations can be directed toward the temples or the center of the forehead to initiate third eye stimulation. As always, whenever using power objects such as these, call upon your higher guidance and visually surround yourself and your partner with light.

Azurite nodules, or healing stones, can be placed over any part of the body where there is physical blockage or congestion. As the Azurite ray penetrates and moves the energy, it is very likely that the psychic-emotional reasons for the physical blockage will surface into the mind. As this occurs, it may become necessary to lend assistance in counseling or meditation to release the roots of the blockage.

BLOODSTONE

In Bloodstone, the deep earth green and equally deep blood red combine together to create a very powerful cleanser for the physical body. This stone is an important healer, for it purifies the blood and strengthens the blood purifying organs: kidneys, liver and spleen. There is tremendous power in the combination of red and green, which directs the healing color of green into the bloodstream, often creating a state of detoxification. The stone can be placed upon the body over areas of congestion or sluggish circulation, primarily over the cleansing organs. For persons who have physically and emotionally purified themselves, Bloodstone can assist in transforming the physical vehicle to carry greater amounts of light and energy.

CARNELIAN

Carnelian is one of the most popular stones in the chalcedony family. This red-orange agate is composed of silicon dioxide which is commonly known as quartz. It is one of the most common chemical compounds found on our earth. Carnelian does not form in six-sided terminated crystals, as Clear Quartz and Amethyst does, and vibrates at a lower energy frequency. Still, it deserves the claim of being an important contributor in the Quartz family.

Carnelian, as all agates, has evolved with the cycles of the earth and has become one of the power stones of the ages. Carnelian is the gem of the earth, a symbol of the strength and beauty of our planet. It represents the golden-orange dawns, the red sunsets, the autumn leaves and the deep richness of the fertile ground. It has grown and evolved along with the human race for thousands of years. It can help to teach one how to carve out a unique place in life and how to utilize personal power in the physical world.

Carnelian is not a high-powered energy source and will draw in light for its own purposes. Instead of projecting and emanating that light, as higher vibration transparent stones can do, it reflects back the depth of color of our own physical world. Because Carnelian is indigenous to earth and carries the stories and records of our planet, it can be used (with advanced training) to see into the past.

Carnelian serves as a grounder of energies and as a manifester on the physical plane. It is good for people who are absent minded or confused and unfocused. It grounds the attention into the present moment so that one can concentrate upon current happenings and thus become more productive. When used in meditation, it helps to focus the mind on higher intentions and goals.

It is a good stone to place around the navel and pelvic area for infertility or impotency. The red-orange color stimulates the sexual chakra and assists in blood purification to cleanse the reproductive organs of any physical energy blockages that could prevent successful procreation.

Carnelian is carved into beautiful jewelry and religious medallions. It is often worn in medicine bags and amulets by those wishing to use its energy for protection. Carnelian stimulates a deeper love and appreciation for the beauty and gifts of the earth.

LAPIS

Lapis is one of the power stones of the ages. The deep royal blue with bright gold flecks has always been a symbol of power and royalty. In ancient Egypt it was known as the color of the gods and revered as a messenger from the heavens. In the great barren dry land in which Egyptians lived, this deep cobalt blue color was a great contrast to their arid desert tones and hues. The gold flecks were like the stars in their night-time sky and they were regarded as touchstones for truth and light. Egyptians believed that by meditating upon these colors they could touch the hem of God's infinite robe.

The stone was often ground and made into dyes that colored the robes and garments of the high priests and those of royal blood. By wearing this color, Egyptians felt that they became a representative of the Gods and that supernatural forces would empower their lives. Lapis was also pulverized, used as remedies for certain maladies and as a contra-indicator for poisons. It was thought that this deep blue power of God would cleanse the system and make it free of impurities and toxins. Egyptians believed that the soul existed in the mind and was housed in the brain, and Lapis-blue became the mental healer and soul purifier. Lapis was used to purge the soul of demonic possession by pulverizing the stone, mixing it with gold, making it into a poultice and placing it upon the crown of the head. As it dried it would draw out the demons and cleanse the soul's impurities. In extreme cases a small hole was drilled in the skull and the Lapis mixture was poured into the head of the possessed.

Today Lapis serves as both a mental and spiritual cleanser. It can be consciously used in certain circumstances by highly evolved souls to purge or cleanse the aura of a part of the past that is no longer necessary to carry. Lapis can be placed upon the third eye area to penetrate through subconscious blockages in order to contact the intuitive neutral mind. Lapis will assist one to develop the stability and power of mind through which the soul force can function. Lapis draws the mind inward to seek its own source of power. In this process often there are many old memory patterns with charged emotional wounds that need to be released and healed. Lapis penetrates rather than heals. Therefore, it is advisable to use a specific healing stone in conjunction with Lapis when doing this kind of work (Green Aventurine, Rose Quartz, Amethyst). Lapis represents going through your own darkness and illusion, your own subconscious, to truly identify with your own God Self. The flecks of gold symbolize the wisdom that is achieved upon completing this process.

MALACHITE

I am Malachite, the green fire, septor of the fourth ray. I am the dragon, satan fear, the lizard, the serpent, the frog, the dense; you know me in your modest dreams. . . .

I am the wheel, the hub—the unfolding universe. I am the black void, density in manifestation. I am the womb of creation.

I am what is yet unknown, uncreated, unmanifest within you.

I am old, you have known me since time began. I am the original thought, the original purpose.

Summary Important Healing Stones

You must work with me and through me. Some say "I am dense" and therefore unappealing, yet you must overcome density as long as you endure on this planet. How else shall you understand the nature of spirit and spiritual law unless you create with the material realm?

There is no part of your body that remains untouched by me, for I am creativity, the essence of alterability within you.

My mask is blackness, my purpose is creation, I am the womb, the mystic pool.

Do not seek in total to understand me, my essence is unfathomable. I am the deepest yearning in your heart, the deepest fear in your mind, the ultimate process of experience—CREATION.

Use the power of the I AM wisely. I am malachite.

Written by Gary Fleck

Malachite is one of the oldest known stones and has been used for thousands of years for its healing and transforming properties. In ancient Egyptian times Malachite was used by the upper classes as one of their main power stones. It served as a grounding force to help them channel higher energies onto the planet. The pharaohs often lined the inside of their headdresses with Malachite and believed that it helped them to rule wisely. The stone was also pulverized into a powder and used on the eyes for poor eyesight, inner vision and also for cosmetic purposes.

Malachite can serve different purposes for different people. If someone is very evolved and dedicated to humanitarian purposes, Malachite assists in grounding higher energies onto the planet to be used for these purposes. For those who are in a purification process, Mal-

143

achite acts as a purger and a mirror to the subconscious, reflecting into the conscious mind that which needs to be cleansed.

Malachite personifies the deep healing green of nature and represents innate beauty of the earth-herbs, flowers, trees, roots and plants. It manifests a deep devic green which rules the material plane. This stone is dense and nontransparent, and absorbs energy instead of emitting it. It is therefore good to place Malachite stones over areas that are dis-eased or painful to draw out the negative energy and surface the psychic-emotional reasons for it. Because of the absorbing properties, it is important to cleanse these stones after being used, for they can become dull and lifeless and lose their power if they take on too much negative energy. The most effective way to cleanse Malachite is by placing it on a larger quartz cluster for at least three hours. It can also be purified by the water/sun method (see Care of Stones, Chapter 2). It is not advisable to use salt for cleansing Malachite because it is a very soft material and can scratch easily.

Great movement, flow and energy exist in the lines, circles and designs that comprise the endless creative patterns inherent in Malachite. Many stories are told by the pictures found in Malachite that reveal the message and purpose of the stone itself. For example, a stone that on one side has two circles coming together and on the other side has only one circle, could be used to harmonize duality within one's self or within a relationship. Malachite, which may or may not contain symbols or pictures, can be tuned into by placing the stone to the third eye and intuitively or visually receiving the message the stone has to relay. The bullseye design found in Malachite is a powerful focusing tool and can be placed on the third eye for inner vision or concentration during meditation. Bullseye stones can also be placed over any part of the body or chakra system that needs to be opened up to circulate more energy. Malachite stones that have straight lines will move energy in the direction that the lines are placed.

Malachite is like a good, honest friend—one that will tell you the truth about yourself and help bring to the surface that which is unknown or unseen to your own conscious mind. Because of the ability to surface that which is not evident, Malachite has often been tabooed as a healing stone. When used, worn or meditated upon, Malachite will draw out, surface and reflect that which is impeding spiritual growth. Therefore, Malachite should always be used with respect and with an awareness of the cleansing effects involved. This power stone is best used in conjunction with meditation to help balance and release the debris that Malachite will surface.

Malachite is an all purpose healing stone and can be used over any of the chakras or any part of the body. However, it serves best over the solar plexus to clear static or repressed emotions. When the solar plexus is cleared and open, energy can move freely between the upper and lower chakras. When placed directly over the solar plexus point, tension is released from the diaphragm and deep complete breathing restored. This balances the energy between the heart center and the navel chakra, creating a physical and emotional state of well being. When Malachite blends with other minerals, it changes its character and no longer manifests the defined lines, circles and patterns that it does when expressing its own true nature. As in all relationships, it must yield a part of its own identity in order to merge with another stone. Because Malachite is such a congenial partner, it is able to surrender itself to enter into a meaningful union with the two main stones that are willing partners: Azurite and Chrysocolla. Both Azurite and Chrysocolla manifest different hues of blue, each with the capacity to merge with Malachite's powerful earth green. Uniting, new entities are created—ones that inherit their own characteristics and purpose.

MALACHITE-AZURITE

When Malachite and Azurite unite together, the deep blue of Azurite is softened by the healing green tones of Malachite and thus creates a stone with increased healing powers. Malachite gives up a bit of its probing abilities to yield to the deep Azurite blue and relinquishes some of its power and clarity of definition, creating a lighter and more calming ray.

This stone combination can be used in all cases where either Malachite or Azurite alone would be placed over a blocked or congested area. Working together results in increased healing and assimilation. Azurite by itself penetrates and moves energy. With its Malachite-mate this process becomes more grounded and integrated. Malachite-Azurite calms the state of anxiety that usually accompanies physical dis-ease so that the healing process can occur. The blending of blue and green soothes and makes this healing possible. The blue calms the stress so that the healing green can go to work on the physical level. Working as a unit, the blue penetrates and the green initiates the healing force. Malachite-Azurite acts as a blanket that could be wrapped around someone, creating comfort to allow the healing process to occur.

When used over the third eye to cleanse the subconscious, it is likely that many past thoughts and feelings will enter the awareness. These emotionally charged thoughts can then be neutralized and released, creating a higher and clearer mental state. Azurite alone will penetrate through negative mental states (depression, anxiety, etc.) to initiate an intuitive experience. Malachite-Azurite helps to establish that experience as a personal reality instead of a transitory state.

When using this stone on yourself or others, be prepared for emotional releases and physical detoxification. Be ready to guide yourself or your partner through the cleansing process which may involve counseling, meditation, empathy or hugs.

MALACHITE-CHRYSOCOLLA

The marriage between Malachite and Chrysocolla is indeed a special union. Malachite's deep earth green and the sky blue of Chrysocolla blend harmoniously together to create an obvious balance of the bluegreen color spectrum. In the presence of the feminine energies of Chrysocolla, Malachite softens its force, often to the point of becoming translucent or neon. Chrysocolla also surrenders aspects of its nature in becoming passive to Malachite. In so doing, Chrysocolla has the potential to raise in vibration to manifest a gem quality transparency. When this happens the healing power is increased as light is then able to shine completely through the stone. In yielding and blending together, both stones raise their frequency to a level that is rarely accomplished alone. Harmonizing their talents, Malachite-Chrysocolla offers a unique service for personal and planetary renewal.

These stones symbolize wholeness and often resemble small earths—with the land and water represented by the greens and blues. It is extremely beneficial to place them on larger Clear Quartz clusters as a prayer for world peace is offered. In this way, the generating energies of quartz will continue to project the mental image of peace long after the prayer is given.

When Malachite-Chrysocolla is worn or placed over an imbalanced area, it lends its sense of peace and wellness and communicates the message of wholeness to the body. Having sensed this, the cells and internal tissues respond to the subtle stimulus and strive to align themselves with this image of harmony. When these stones are placed over the third eye area the mind becomes calm and negative thought patterns are neutralized. By placing one on the third eye and one at the solar plexus, the mind and body come into alignment. This establishes a rapport that enables one to communicate with greater clarity and compassion.

Malachite is the healing green of the earth and Chrysocolla the infinite blue of the summer sky. By combining earth and ether energies together this stone can serve to balance and integrate the physical with the spiritual, creating a sense of wholeness and well-being.

MOONSTONE

Moonstone helps to soothe and balance the emotions. When emotional reactions prevail, it is difficult to connect with the higher planes of reality. As Malachite brings the subconscious out, Moonstone balances, soothes and heals, so that one is not living and identifying in an emotional state. Moonstones assist the mastery of emotions by bringing them under the control of Higher Will instead of repressing or expressing them. Many old emotional patterns are stored in the subconscious. Moonstone acts as a guardian at the gateway to the subconscious and serves to protect us from our own emotions. This in turn allows a greater awareness to unfold. Moonstones can be placed at the center of the chi (the Moon Center) to create this balance. They are also very useful for women at the time of their menstrual cycle to assist in physical hormonal and emotional equilibrium. They also help men to become more in-tune with the feminine aspect of their nature. Moonstones epitomize the astrological sign of Libra, the ultimate balance achieved by neutralizing negative emotions. These stones are a gift, allowing one to experience calmness and peace of mind. Once that experience is obtained and becomes a part of our nature, the fear of feeling is neutralized and emotional balance achieved.

PERIDOT

Peridot manifests one of nature's most clear and vibrant green colors. The vibration is not as high or intense as some of the other stones in the green spectrum. Mal-

149

achite and Emerald also display this color, but the green found in these stones blends more of the blue color ray than that of Peridot. Green-blue stones will direct energy toward the mental, emotional and spiritual levels while greater amounts of yellow will bring the healing green into the physical plane. Because of the larger amount of yellow inherent within Periodot, it directly affects the solar-plexus and navel area which is ruled by the yellow-green energies. Peridot is an earth-plane green which will initiate healing within the physical body. By placing Peridot over the solar plexus, nervous emotional tension known as the "butterflies" can be relaxed and released. It also assists in balancing the endocrine system, especially the adrenal glands, which govern the health of the physical body and are directly associated with the chakras. Peridot acts as a tonic to liven and quicken the entire system, to make it stronger, healthier and more radiant.

Yellow is also the color that is often associated with the mind and the intellect. Peridot is capable of affecting certain negative emotional states such as anger or jealousy. It can cleanse and heal hurt feelings, bruised egos and even assist to mend damaged relationships.

Peridot's most abundant and popular time was during the 1930's and 40's. Its healing energy surfaced during World War II to assist the millions of people who were suffering the mental anguish of heavy war times. It was also a stone that was realatively inexpensive and affordable in economically depressed times.

Wearing or envisioning the vibrant chartreuse of Peridot is mentally stimulating and physically regenerating.

Peridot is still as radiant and rejuvenating today as it was fifty years ago and still serves much the same purpose. It is a good stone to give people who cannot relate to realities beyond the physical world. It will aid physical development and well being.

SELENITE

Natural high quality Selenite crystals possess one of the clearest transparency qualities found in the mineral kingdom. This degree of clarity reflects a pure beam of white light into any environment that the crystal is placed in. When Selenite crystals are used as personal meditation pieces, they will bring into conscious understanding one's own sense of inner truth. Therefore, Selenite can be used to calm and clear troubled or confused states of mind. White is the color vibration associated with the crown chakra. Selenite can be used in meditation or crystal healings to activate this highest of energy centers. A small Selenite crystal can be placed on top of the head to stimulate brain activity and expand the awareness. Selenite symbolizes the clearest state of mind attainable, in which all thoughts entering the consciousness originate from the source and are direct reflections of pure spirit. Selenite is a crystal that can be used for the advancement of the mind and mental powers. It does not serve much purpose in healing the denser physical or emotional bodies.

Some Selenite crystals contain fine linear inclusions within the crystal. These thin striations are like the lines in a book that tell the story of the messages recorded within. These messages may be the earth's own recorded history that Selenite crystals have been exposed to. The records also may be data that has been intentionally projected and stored by ancient magicians and alchemists when their existence was being threatened. In those dark times when they were being burned as witches and driven away as heretics, they chose to preserve their knowledge, wisdom, chemical compounds and alchemical secrets inside Selenite crystals to be retrieved at a future time. They believed that at the right place and time, the right person would sense the treasures contained within, attune their mind to the crystal, and perceive the recorded mysteries. In this way these masters of white magic could continue to carry on the teachings to deserving students, who by their own intuitive attunement earned the right to receive the knowledge.

Because Selenite possesses the ability to record information, it can be used for telepathic communication by people of like-mindedness. One person can beam a specific thought or message into the crystal which the second party attunes to and receives. This type of futuristic communication through thought transference could be used in cases where information is not meant for anyone else or when secrecy is needed. Working with Selenite in this way helps one develop intuitive telepathic powers. In order for Selenite to be used in this way, the crystals have to be exceptionally clear and cleansed after each projected thought.

Since Selenite crystals contain impressions of events that have happened in their presence, they can be used in cases where the truth of a situation needs to be known. For example, if a burglary has occurred in the presence of a Selenite crystal, the crystal can be tuned into, to discover who has committed the theft.

Selenite is an important contributing member of the mineral kingdom and can be used as a touchstone for mental clarity and for developing telepathic powers, as well as appreciated for its inherent beauty.

SODALITE

Sodalite is one of the awakeners of the third eye which prepares the mind to receive the inner sight and intuitive knowledge. Sodalite is the densest and the most grounded of the deep blue stones and elicits deep thought by clearing the mind so that it can function properly. When the mind is calmed and stilled, greater perspective and understanding can be gained. Sodalite lends to the mind the ability to think rationally and intellectually and come to logical conclusions. This is an extremely good stone for those who tend to be oversensitive and reactive because it stabilizies mental power and allows a person to make the shift from emotional to rational. This is a good stone to carry, hold, meditate with or place upon the third eye area to gain intellectual understanding of one's self or a situation. When the mind is balanced and a greater knowledge gained, it then becomes possible to have a greater perspective on life. Sodalite helps clear old mental patterns from the subconscious to make way for conscious thinking. This stone is like the deep dark blue of the night-time sky, when one travels deep within the mind, as in sleep, and returns refreshed with greater understanding and perspective. The white lines and flecks in Sodalite symbolize the spiritual light that comes when one has balanced the mind.

CHAPTER VI
Charts
Resources

The Astrological Trinities Chart is designed to assist individuals in channeling the positive effects and energies of the planets and their associated astrological signs. If intense transits, squares, trines or oppositions are occurring in one's chart, the stones associated with those planets and signs can be worn or worked with to assist in learning the lessons those conjuncts offer. If planets are squaring one another or are in opposition, stones associated with each planet can be worn separately for equal amounts of time to balance the effects. When trines, sextiles or conjunctions occur, associated stones can be worn together to harmonize each of the planets' energies. When trying to attune to the effects and influences of individual planets, specific stones can be worn to direct that energy into your life. If you are not astrologically aware, stones can be worn or meditated with to help you get more in tune with the energies and influences of the planets associated with those stones.

ASTROLOGICAL TRINITIES

CHAKRA	PLANETARY INFLUENCES	ASSOCIATED ASTROLOGICAL SIGN	COLOR	STONE TRINITIES	PURPOSES
First	Pluto	Scorpio	Black	Obsidian	Awakening of dormant unmanifested potential
				Smokey Quartz	Balance of spirit on earth
Base	Mars	Aries	Deep Red	Bloodstone	Cleansing, energizing of physical vehicle
Second	Pluto	Scorpio	Red	Garnet	Utilization of creative energy
				Ruby	Creative energy devoted to highest aspects of self
Creative	Mars	Aries	Orange	Carnelian	Grounding energies into physical
Third	Sun	Leo	Orange	Sulphur	Creates physical radiance

CHAKRA	PLANETARY INFLUENCES	ASSOCIATED ASTROLOGICAL SIGN	COLOR	STONE TRINITIES	PURPOSES
Navel			Yellow	Citrine	Develop self-discipline to live in higher awareness
				Topaz	Confidence in expressing creative power
Solar Plexus	Saturn	Capricorn	Yellow Green	Malachite	Emotional responsibility and balance
				Peridot	Strengthening/regeneration of body
				Green Tourmaline	Strengthen physical to utilize greater spirit force
Fourth Heart	Lower Octave Moon	Cancer	Transition Stones	Rhodochrocite	Move energy—heart to navel
				Moonstone	Balance of emotions
				Opal	Conscious intention of emotions

CHAKRA	PLANETARY INFLUENCES	ASSOCIATED ASTROLOGICAL SIGN	COLOR	STONE TRINITIES	PURPOSES
	Higher Octave: Venus	Taurus	Green	Rose Quartz	Development of self-love
		Libra	Pink	Kunzite	Activation of heart chakra
				Pink Tourmaline	Expression of love in life through sharing
Fifth	Lower Octave: Mercury	Virgo	Blue	Amazonite	Perfecting personal expression
		Gemini		Turquoise	Clarity in communication
				Chrysocholla	Speaking one's own Truth
Throat	Higher Octave: Uranus	Aquarius		Celestite	Attunes one to higher mind
				Aquamarine	Expressing universal truths
				Gem-Silica	Consciously channel higher realms

CHAKRA	PLANETARY INFLUENCES	ASSOCIATED ASTROLOGICAL SIGN	COLOR	STONE TRINITIES	PURPOSES
Sixth Third Eye	Lower Octave: Jupiter Higher Octave: Neptune	Sagittarius Pisces	Indigo Purple	Sodolite Lapis Azurite Sugilite Flourite Amethyst	Understand nature of one's self in relationship to universe Penetrates illusion of the mind Dissolves limited concepts Understand divine purpose Utilization of visionary insight Surrender mind to highest part of one's self
Seventh Crown	Trans-Pluto	Higher Octave: Taurus	White Clear	Selenite Quartz Diamond	Clarity of mind Activities of crown chakra Identification with the immortal part of one's self

159

TABLE 6.2. SUMMARY OF REMAINING HEALING STONES

ADVENTURINE	(Green)	Exemplifies healing green of heart chakra
AMAZONITE	(Blue/Green)	Grounding personal expression
APATITE	(Yellow)	Enhances flow of communication
BLUE LACE AGATE		Peaceful melodious flow of expression
CALCITE	(Yellow)	Memory, greater intellectual capacity
CELESTITE	(Lt. Blue)	Attunes one to higher realms
CHRYSOPRASE	(Green)	To manifest earth plane power
DIOPTASE	(Green)	Rejuvenation of heart chakra
GARNET	(Red)	Creates stimulation of blood flow
IVORY		Grounds physical assertiveness
OPAL		Conscious intention of emotional use
ONYX	(Black)	Root chakra energy
	(Brown)	Grounds connection with the earth
PEARL		Emotional balance and stability
RHODONITE	(Pink/Black)	To actualize ones potential
SULPHUR	(Yellow)	Creates physical radiance
TOPAZ	(Gold)	Conscious connection and manifestation of wisdom
TURQUOISE		Balanced emotional expression

WULFENITE	(Orange)	Energizes and purifies physical body
BERYL FAMILY		
AQUAMARINE	(Blue)	Expressing universal Truths
HELIODORE	(Gold)	Connects one with wisdom of high self
MORGANITE	(Pink)	Purifies and softens high heart octave
GEM FAMILY		
RUBY		Creative energy devoted to God
EMERALD		Powerful subtle body healing
SAPPHIRE		Enlightened intuition
DIAMOND		Personal identification with Infinity
JADE FAMILY		The Dream Stone
RED/GOLD		Receiving master teachings through dreams
LAVENDER		Psychic understanding of dreams
JADEITE	(Light)	Emotional release through dreams
IMPERIAL	(Dark)	Prophetic dreams enacted on physical level

161

TABLE 6.3 COLOR CHAKRA STONES

CHAKRA	PHYSICAL	GLAND	COLOR	STONES	ENERGY
1st. Muladhara	Anus Rectum Colon	Adrenals	Black Red	Blk. Tourmaline Obsidian Bl. Onyx Smokey Q. Bloodstone Realgar Rhodonite Garnet	Ground spirit forces in body. Gain ability to work lovingly on the physical plane.
2nd. Svadhishthana	Pelvic cavity Reproductive organs	Ovaries Prostate Testicle	Red Orange	Ruby Wulfenite Carnelian Citrine Amber	Utilization of creative forces into all aspects of being. High soul procreation. Direct self toward devotion.
3rd. Manipura	Abdominal cavity	Spleen	Orange Yellow	Citrine Topaz	Assimilation of experience. Digestion.

CHAKRA	PHYSICAL GLAND	COLOR	STONES	ENERGY
	Navel Digestive organs		Apatite Sulphur Calcite	Positive use of personal power. Manifest goals.
4th Anahata	Thorasic cavity Heart Rib cage Lungs	Thymus	Green Pink	Adventurine Peridot Malachite Emerald Dioptase Gr. Tourmaline Rhodochrocite Rose Quartz Kunzite Morganite Pk. Tourmaline	Release emotionally suppressed trauma. Soul/heart consciousness. Expressing love in action.

CHAKRA	PHYSICAL GLAND	COLOR	STONES	ENERGY
5th Vishuddha	Throat Voice Neck — Thyroid Para-thyroid	Blue	Bl. LaceAgate Amazonite Celestite Chrysocholla Turquoise Gem Silica Aquamarine	Ability to verbalize. Expressing Truth through power of the spoken word.
6th Ajna	Third-eye Higher brain centers — Pituitary	Indigo Violet	Sodalite Azurite Lapis Sapphire Flourite Sugelite Amethyst	Idigo-clearing sub-conscious to channel intuition. Purple-bal-anced state of mind. See Divine perfection in all things. Devo-tion.
7th Sahasrata	Crown Highest brain centers — Pineal	Gold White	Heloidor G. Topaz Selenite Clear Q. Diamond	Personal identification with Infinite. Oneness with God. Peace. Wisdom.

MAIN CHAKRA POINTS FOR STONE PLACEMENT

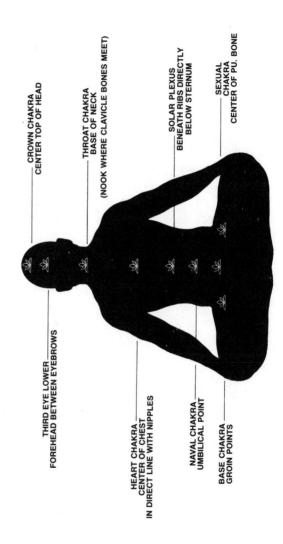

CROWN CHAKRA
CENTER TOP OF HEAD

THROAT CHAKRA
BASE OF NECK
(NOOK WHERE CLAVICLE BONES MEET)

SOLAR PLEXUS
BENEATH RIBS DIRECTLY
BELOW STERNUM

SEXUAL CHAKRA
CENTER OF PU. BONE

THIRD EYE LOWER
FOREHEAD BETWEEN EYEBROWS

HEART CHAKRA
CENTER OF CHEST
IN DIRECT LINE WITH NIPPLES

NAVAL CHAKRA
UMBILICAL POINT

BASE CHAKRA
GROIN POINTS

ACKNOWLEDGMENTS

Linda Bauer, Kelly Mattsson	Typing
Kevin Braheny	Model for back cover
JaneAnn Dow	Collaboration, support, encouragement
Gary Fleck	Chrysocolla and Malachite poems
Anand Singh Khalsa	Back Cover Photo
Rapa H. S. Khalsa	Love and Support
Ben Levine, Shirin Strauss	Editing
Charles Meidzinski	Consultation and information
ORION	The source of information contained in this book
Sananda Ra	Inspiration
Eric Starwalker Rubel	Astrological consultation
Barbara Somerfield	For coming into my life and making this book a reality

RECOMMENDED READING

Cosmic Crystals	By Ra Bonewitz
Exploring Atlantis	
Volumes I and II	By Frank Alper
Gemstones of the World	By Walter Schumann
Gem Therapy	By A. K. Bhattacharya
Healing Stoned	By Joel Glick and Gloria Lorusso

Katrina Raphaell is available for lectures, classes and workshops. To facilitate immediate use of crystal healing techniques, quartz crystals, beginning and advanced sets of healing stones and many of the individual stones discussed in this book are available from:

KATRINA RAPHAELL
P.O. BOX 3208
TAOS, NEW MEXICO 87571

GLOSSARY

AURA—the electro-magnetic field surrounding life forms; the soul's light force as it manifests through the body; the extended energy around the human body which alters in radiance and color depending upon the state of physical, mental, emotional and spiritual health.

CAUSAL PLANE—the primal level of thought when pure spirit lowers its frequency to creatively express in the conception of ideas; thought that is consciously aligned with and utilizing the cosmic force; the mental blueprint for physical manifestation.

CHAKRA—energy centers in the human body that are associated with various states of evolution, consciousness, physical organs, glands, colors and stones; any one of seven main energy centers in the body.

CRYSTALS—nature's three-dimensional geometric forms whose outward appearance mirrors the internalized perfect ordering of atoms. The unity among the particles comprising crystals vibrate with a cosmic harmony which can be tapped into and used in healing or in the evolution of consciousness. Crystals are capable of reflecting pure light and color that can be channeled in numerous ways.

DIMENSION—a state of reality; a level of existence; a realm of consciousness; infinite in number with each successive dimension forming the foundation for the progressive evolution of the next.

168

ENERGY CENTER—an area in the human body that has increased vital force, usually a nerve plexus, accupressure point or chakra.

ENERGY VORTEX (VORTEX OF ENERGY)—a powerful spiraling force created by placing specific stone combinations over chakra centers or by using crystals in any number of ways; an opening of the ethers to channel cosmic forces onto the earth plane.

ETHERS, ETHERIC PLANE, ETHERICALLY—the non-physical realities existing in the higher dimensions; the spiritual realms inhabited by beings of a more celestial strain; pertaining to those realms.

GREAT CENTRAL SUN—the omnipotent eternal source of light existing in the center of the infinite universe out of which radiates the entire panoramic creation; the power that creates the infinite universe.

HEALING STONES—any natural precious or semi-precious stones, rocks or crystals whose healing properties are known and used to balance, restore or maintain physical mental emotional or spiritual wellness.

HIGHER CONSCIOUSNESS, HIGHER MIND, HIGHER SELF—attuned and aligned with the source of power and truth within the Self; the neutral aspect of awareness that identifies with spiritual light and is fulfilled by creatively manifesting that light through thoughts, feelings, words and actions.

HIGHER ENERGIES—pertaining to the soul, truth, love and positive forces.

LOWER CONSCIOUSNESS, LOWER MIND, LOWER SELF—unawakened to soul qualities and energies; existing in the unfulfilled desire state; seeking fulfillment solely from external sources; egocentric, caring only for the self; consumed and indulgent with sensory gratification and transitory pleasure.

LOWER ENERGIES—pertaining to the unevolved egocentric nature or negative forces.

MATERIAL, PHYSICAL, OR EARTH PLANE—that aspect of creation that exists in slow moving time and space in which the illusion of form is created.

MINERALS—the natural chemical elements or compounds that occur in nature and form the earth's crust.

OVERSOUL, OVERSOUL BEINGS—those who exist in the etheric planes and are aligned and attuned to the source of spiritual light; those serving as non-physical spiritual guides and friends in the evolutionary process of individuals and of the planet; advanced beings who originally inhabited the earth and seeded the root races; those forming the brotherhood of light.

PLANE—a level of existance, a realm of consciousness; a dimension of reality.

PRECIOUS STONES—multi-colored crystalline gemstones that usually display transparency and are capable of reflecting high amounts of light and pure rays of color; stones best used when trying to affect or heal the subtle bodies; rubies, emeralds, diamonds, sapphires, aquamarine, topaz etc.

RADIATED—a process by which crystals are exposed to intense amounts of x-rays which alters the molecular structure and changes the natural form of color; clear quartz crystals radiated to exemplify smoky quartz.

SEMI-PRECIOUS STONES—any number of multi-colored stones, usually dull opaque and nontransparent; stones reflecting colors and energies that are best used when trying to affect or heal physical, subconscious or emotional imbalances; turquoise, lapis, agate, malachite, etc.

SOUL—the spark of infinite spirit existing within each individual; that which holds the key to ultimate truth and power; the unique personalized aspect of the cosmic force.

SPIRIT—the omnipresent intelligent life force comprising and creating all manifest and non-manifest states of reality; the cosmic force which is eternally existent, changeless and true; the common denominator throughout the entire creation; the spark of life, the light, the truth and the source of all that is.

STAR CHILDREN—those beings incarnated on the earth that originate from other planets and/or galaxies; those lightworkers who have come to teach the higher laws and principles of the universe.

SUBTLE BODIES—those aspects of the human being that are not physical yet authentic; those more refined and etheric qualities; the mental body, the auric body, the astral body, the soul body, etc.

TERMINATE, TERMINATED—to come to a point; to reach completion at the apex; when the faces of a crystal meet together to form the top peak.

WALK-INS—an advanced soul that transfers its identity into an adult body in which the previously existing soul occupant no longer wishes to inhabit; an evolved being whose purpose it is to teach and share spiritual light.

AURORA PRESS

THE ELISABETH HAICH SERIES

Through books such as *Initiation*, Elisabeth Haich has become world famous for her profound understanding of the human soul. The Yoga schools she set up in Europe with Selvarajan Yesudian have become internationally renowned.

WISDOM OF THE TAROT

Wisdom of the Tarot relates the path of higher consciousness through the color, shape and symbolic forms on the 22 cards. Detailed study of a Tarot card may release instinctive awareness of each level towards the Light. When studied individually, a card may reveal the necessary steps to find one's essential path. Included are 5 color gold Tarot cards.
Paper 174pp.   **$12.50**

SEXUAL ENERGY & YOGA

This book is to introduce the concept of transmuting the physical emotional psychic mental energy people normally disperse in sexual activity for the purpose of uniting their bodies in their higher Self or God.
Paper 160pp   **$6.95**

SELF HEALING, YOGA AND DESTINY

Designed to reconnect you with the Divine, the concepts within this book explain the attitudes necessary for the path back to one's Self. Based on many years personal experience, the author creates a vehicle to realize the essential source of Life, especially in relation to illness and self healing.
Paper 80pp.   **$4.95**

THE DAY WITH YOGA

A different creative energy is at work on each day of the week. In this book Elisabeth Haich has carefully chosen and collected quotations which show us how we can attune to the cosmic vibrations of each day.
Paper 96pp.   **$3.95**

THE EAR

Gateway to Balancing the Body
A Modern Guide to Ear Acupuncture
Mario Wexu, D. Ac.

This is the first complete modern textbook of ear acupuncture. Anatomical descriptions with detailed charts clearly illustrate how to locate and use over 300 ear points, both alone and in combination with body points, to treat and prevent illness. An excellent repertory listing 150 diseases facilitates an indepth understanding of this incredible and valuable healing art.
Cloth 203pp.   **$30.00**

COLOR THERAPY

Dr. Reuben Amber

This comprehensive book enumerates the myriad ways we can consciously choose to use color to influence our body, mind, and soul to promote balanced health and well being. No other book includes as thorough a historical survey of Color Therapies along with specific applications of color in all facets of life.
Paper 207pp.   **$9.95**

HOW ATMOSPHERIC CONDITIONS AFFECT YOUR HEALTH

Dr. Michel Gauquelin

A unique exploration by psychologist and statistician Dr. Michel Gauquelin, of the tremendous influence of the cycle of the seasons, range of climates, cosmic clocks, Lunar Cycles, & Sunspots on the complex balance of mental and physical health.
Paper 224pp.   **$8.95**

CHART INTERPRETATION —

Astrology and Psychology
Doris Hebel

A compilation of articles on Chart Interpretation, covering Elements, aspects, hemisphere emphasis, retrogrades, stations, parental indicators, and case histories.
Paper 64pp.   **$5.**

SYNASTRY

Understanding Human Relations
Through Astrology *Ronald Davison*

This book contains the first comprehensive survey of the various techniques of horoscope comparison.

The author has discovered "The Relationship Horoscope," an entirely new way of charting in a single horoscope the relationship between two people. He also introduces new methods of determining the quality of that relationship.
Paper 352pp.   **$10.95**

AWAKEN SELF-HEALING ENERGY THROUGH THE TAO

Mantak Chia

This unique book reveals the ancient Taoist secret of circulating internal energy through acupuncture meridians, for physical, psychological and spiritual health. Written in clear, easy to understand language and illustrated with many detailed diagrams that aid the development of a powerful energetic flow.
Paper 224pp.   **$10.95**